JOB MATTERS

ELEKTROTECHNIK

Michael Benford
Wolf-Rainer Windisch

VERITAS
Cornelsen

Bildnachweis

CV-Archiv:	S. 11/4,6
IstockImages:	S. 11/2,3
ShutterstockImages:	S. 7/1–4, 6–7, S. 11/1,5,7, S. 24/1–8, S. 37, S. 39
Fotofinder:	S. 14/DenkouImages
GettyImages:	S. 7/5 RF, S. 11/8
PictureAlliance:	S. 4/W.Fiedler, S. 29/dpa

Oxford Designers and Illustrators, Oxford	Alle Grafiken

Nicht alle Copyright-Inhaber konnten ermittelt werden; deren Urheberrechte werden hiermit vorsorglich und ausdrücklich anerkannt.

Contents

Reference

What is electricity?

Lightning: 10^9 volts (up to 1 gigavolt)

T2 **1 Read the following dialogue and listen to it on the CD. Then make a list of any words you don't understand and look them up.**

Trainee: What exactly is electricity?

Instructor: Well, to understand electricity you first have to understand the difference between voltage and current. Do you know anything about them?

Trainee: Well, everybody knows that that the voltage in the mains is 230V and current means something that flows.

Instructor: Exactly. Electricity flows along a conductor, like copper wire. To understand all this let's first look at the basic building block of all things – the atom. What are atoms made of?

Trainee: Things like protons, electrons and neutrons?

Instructor: Very good! Let's look at the electrons and protons. These atomic particles have an electric charge. Protons are positive and electrons are negative. They are opposites and what do you know about opposites?

Trainee: Opposites attract.

Instructor: Exactly. If you separate electrons and protons, a force is produced between them because they want to get back together again. This force is called the potential difference or voltage. A voltage is a force waiting to be set free. In this case, the electrons want to get to the protons. A battery is a good example of this. How do you get power from a battery?

Trainee: You put a load between the positive and negative terminals.

Instructor: And so what do you think flows between the terminals?

Trainee: Electrons. OK, now I understand what current is.

Instructor: Yes, it's a flow of electrons, but to understand it in more detail, imagine that in one terminal of a battery electrons are missing. What is it now – positive or negative?

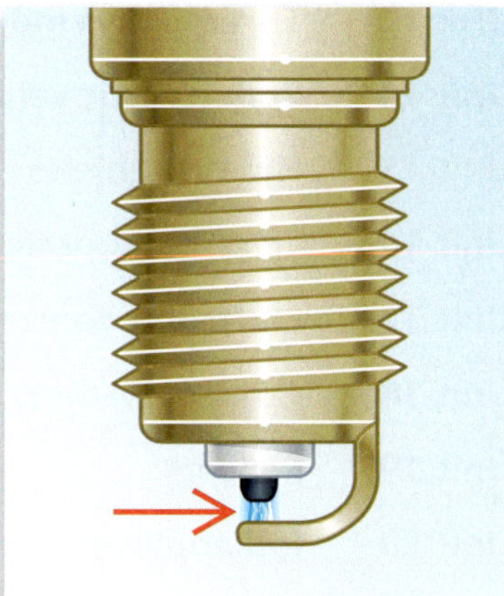

A spark across spark plug terminals: about 20,000V

Trainee: Positive.

Instructor: Very good! The positive terminal has "holes" waiting for electrons. In the other terminal, the negative one, there are lots of extra electrons waiting to get to those holes. If you put a conductor between the two terminals, electrons rush down it to get to the holes and on the way they can power a load, for example a light bulb. Can you think of a good conductor?

Trainee: You mentioned copper a moment ago.

Instructor: Exactly. Copper is a good conductor. Electrons flow along it easily. It has very low resistance. Now let's think of different ways to separate electrons and protons …

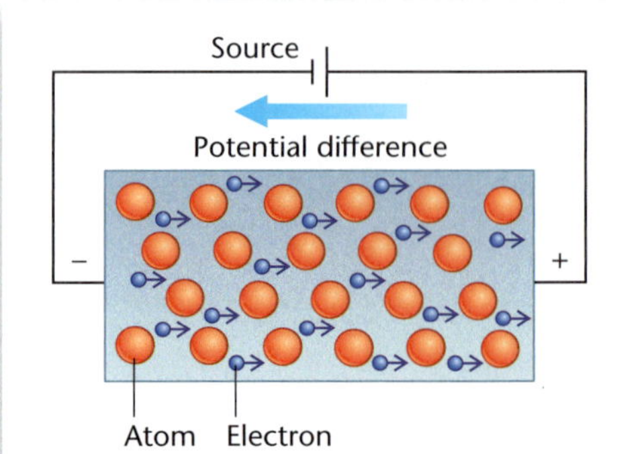

Voltage

is the force which causes a current to flow in a closed electrical circuit. It is symbolized by the letters E or V and is measured in volts (V).

Current

is a flow of charged particles (e.g. electrons). The flow of the current outside the power source is from the plus terminal to the minus one. The electrons move in the opposite direction. The value of the current depends on the number of electrons which pass a fixed point per second. Current is symbolized by the letter I and is measured in amperes or amps (A).

2 Choose the right answer to complete the sentences.

1 A current
- a is always a flow of electrons.
- b is a flow of protons.
- c can be a flow of anything.

2 Voltage
- a is a measure of force.
- b is a measure of resistance.
- c is a measure of current.

3 A potential difference can exist between
- a protons and neutrons.
- b electrons and protons.
- c electrons and neutrons.

4 When electrons and protons are separated
- a the electrons try to get to the protons.
- b the protons become neutrons.
- c the neutrons try to get to the protons.

5 A good conductor
- a has low resistance to protons.
- b has high resistance to electrons.
- c has low resistance to electrons.

Did you know..?

An average bolt of high-voltage lightning has a current of 300 – 500 kiloamperes at a potential difference of up to1 gigavolt (1 billion volts), but it lasts for only 0.0004 seconds. This is just enough energy to light a 100 watt light bulb for about 45 years.

Electric guitar pickups have magnets to generate electricity.

3 Fill in the gaps with words from the dialogue, the definitions and the diagram.

When you connect electrical equipment to the ____________ 1 the ______________ 2 is 230V. The metal most often used as a ____________ 3 is ________________ 4 because it has very low ____________ 5 to electrons. The flow of electrons is called the ____________________ 6 and is measured in ____________ 7. Electricity is normally used to power a _________________ 8, e.g. a motor. The quantity of electrons waiting to flow is the ______________________ 9 difference. It is measured in ____________ 10.

4 Label the three atomic particles in the atom.

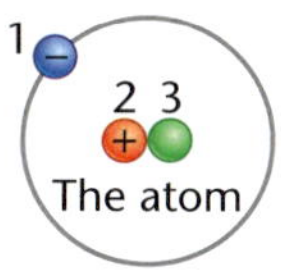

1 ____________
2 ____________
3 ____________

electron • neutron • proton

DC voltage: batteries

1 Read the text and then label the parts of the dry cell battery.

The most common source of direct current is a battery. Zinc-carbon (dry cell) batteries (e.g. AAA, AA, C and D) are the most common type of commercial battery. The **cathode** is a **carbon rod**. It is placed in the middle of a **zinc casing**, which forms the **anode**. The space around it is filled with an **acid paste**. When they are connected by a conductor (e.g. a copper wire), electrons from the anode (zinc) flow along the wire to the cathode (carbon) and produce a current. The zinc of the anode is eaten up by the acid during this reaction and when there is no more zinc left, the battery is dead. In some batteries the chemical reaction can be reversed by an external voltage. These batteries are called rechargeable batteries or accumulators. Unfortunately, they cannot be recharged indefinitely. How often an accumulator can be recharged depends on the technology used. Car batteries using lead and lead-dioxide plates are one of the longest lasting types of accumulator. A further source of DC voltage is photovoltaic cells. Photovoltaic cells are becoming more and more important for generating electricity.

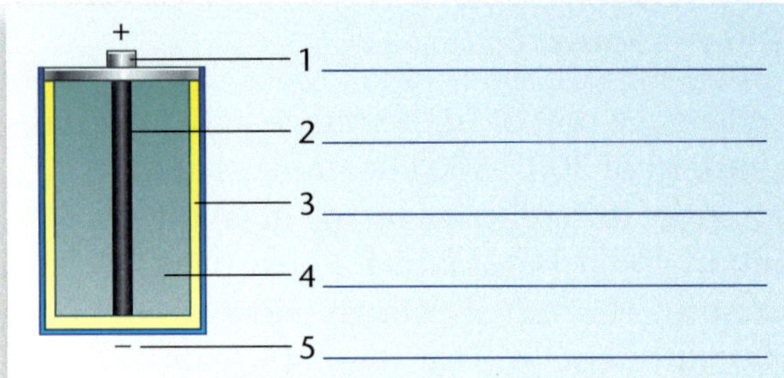

Dry cell battery

2 Study the text and the diagrams and then say if the following statements are true or false. Correct the false statements.

1 A battery produces direct current.
2 The anode of a battery is positive.
3 An anode is often made of copper.
4 Electrons flow from the cathode to the anode.
5 In a zinc-carbon battery the acid paste eats up the carbon.
6 The zinc casing of a dry cell battery is positive.
7 An accumulator is a rechargeable battery.
8 An accumulator can't be recharged very often if it has lead and lead-dioxide plates.
9 A photovoltaic cell is a form of battery.

T3 3 How a simple battery works: Put the sentences in the right order. Start with D. Then listen to the CD and check your sentences.

A "Holes" for the missing electrons are produced in these protons.
B A lead dioxide plate, which is called the cathode, is carefully put into the acid on the other side of the vessel.
C A lead plate, which is called the anode, is carefully put into the acid on one side of the vessel.
D A strong glass vessel is half-filled with sulphuric acid.
E Electricity is generated.
F Electrons in the lead dioxide plate are separated from their protons by a chemical reaction.
G Electrons in the lead plate are freed by the sulphuric acid.
H It can be used to power a load.
I The free electrons from the anode are attracted to the protons with holes in the cathode.
J The two plates are connected by a copper wire.

1 D 2 ___ 3 ___ 4 ___ 5 ___ 6 ___ 7 ___ 8 ___ 9 ___ 10 ___

4 Complete these passive sentences with one of the following words.

connected • eaten • generated • produced • separated • used

1 Electrons are ________________ from the atoms by the acid.
2 The terminals are ______________ by a piece of copper wire.
3 Protons with missing electrons are ________________ by the chemical reaction.
4 The zinc is _________________________ up by the acid.
5 Lead is ________________ by car battery manufacturers.
6 Electricity is _____________ by using photovoltaic cells.

Remember the passive?

They **are connected** by a wire.
The rod **is placed** in the middle.

5 Name the appliances and match them with the batteries.

a

b
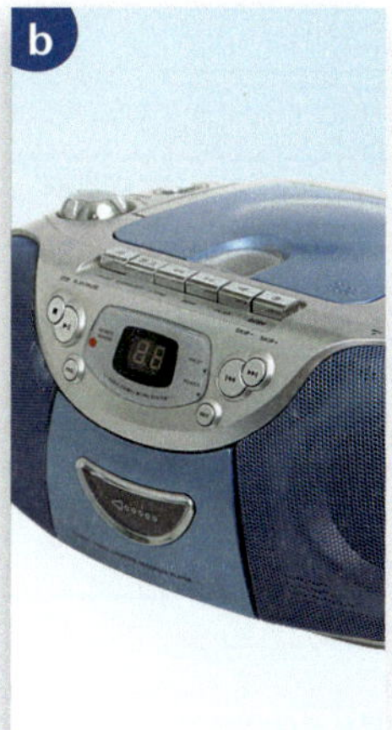

c

Battery types

Voltage	Name	Capacity
12V	car battery	40Ah[1]
9V	PP3 / block battery	400mAh[2]
4.5V	4.5 volt battery	1,800mAh
1.5V	D	12,000mAh
1.5V	C	7,800mAh
1.5V	AA (double A)	2,400mAh
1.5V	AAA (triple A)	1,120mAh
1.5 – 3V	button cell	80mAh

[1] ampere-hour
[2] milliampere-hour

d

e

f

g

h

AC voltage sources: dynamos and generators

1 Use the text and the diagram to complete the sentences below.

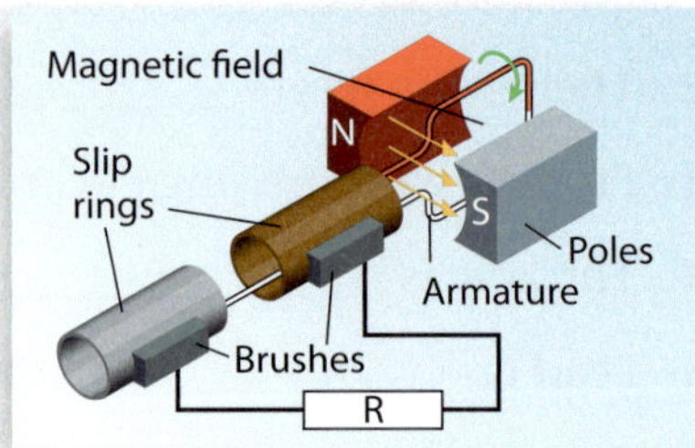

An electric generator has a wire (conductor), wound in loops (armature) which is rotated through the magnetic field of a magnet. Each time the wire moves across the magnetic field, the free electrons move to one end of the wire and produce a voltage (tension). The direction of the movement of electrons changes with the direction of the movement of the wire. In the diagram the circular movement of the armature generates an alternating current (AC). If the ends of the wire are joined together there is a flow of electrons and this generates a current which can power a load. The current in the moving wire also produces its own magnetic field which combines with the magnetic field of the magnet and opposes the movement of the wire (see exercise 4, Lenz's Law).

1 An armature is ______

2 A voltage is only produced when the wire moves ______

3 If the wire moves in a different direction, the electrons ______

4 In the generator shown, alternating current is generated because ______

______

5 A load can be powered if ______

6 A second magnetic field is produced by ______

2 Test your knowledge: Look at the diagram and choose the correct statements.

1 Current flows through the conductor when you move it
a in the direction of the magnetic field (left and right).
b across the magnetic field (up and down).
c in any direction in the magnetic field.

2 The current flows
a in different directions depending on which way the conductor is moved.
b in the same direction no matter which way the conductor is moved.
c only when the conductor is moved downwards.

3 The current is greatest when the conductor
a is moved slowly.
b isn't moved.
c is moved fast.

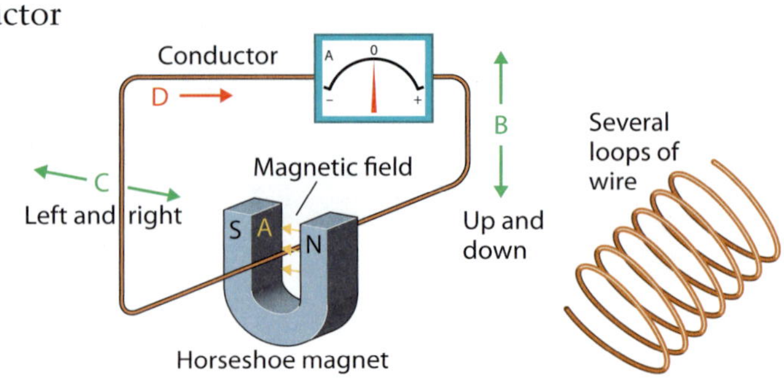

4 If several loops of wire are moved through the magnetic field,
a the current is weaker
b the current is stronger
c it makes no difference

5 If a stronger magnet is used
a the current is weaker b the current is stronger c it makes no difference

3 Use the diagram to complete the explanation below.

When a conductor is moved across a magnetic field, a voltage is induced (generated) in the conductor. The direction in which the ____________________[1] flows in an electric circuit depends on the polarity of the magnetic ____________________[2] and the direction of the ____________________[3].

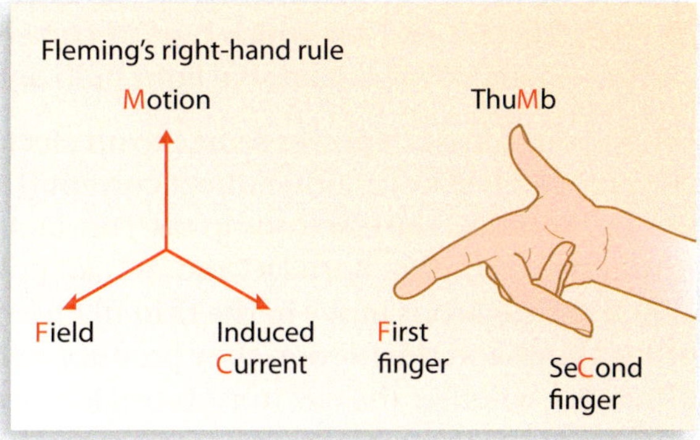

4 Use the following explanation to complete the sentences.

The strength of the voltage depends on **a)** the speed at which the conductor moves across the field (or the magnetic field moves past the conductor); **b)** the strength of the magnetic field; and **c)** the number of loops in the conductor

1 The weaker the magnetic field, **2** The fewer loops the conductor has, **3** The stronger the magnetic field, **4** The faster the conductor moves, **5** The slower the conductor moves, **6** The more loops the conductor has,	the stronger the weaker	the current.

Lenz's Law

The magnetic field induced in a conductor opposes the cause.

T4 5 Listen to the description of the experiment to demonstrate Lenz's Law and fill in the gaps in the text.

For this experiment we need a permanent magnet and a coil, which is a ____________________[1] made up of many turns of ____________________[2] wire. The two ends of the coil are not joined together. First we hold the coil over the magnet and ____________________[3] it between the poles. It falls quickly at the speed of ____________________[4]. Next, we join the ends of the wire together and drop the coil between the poles again. This time it falls slowly and ____________________[5]. Why does it fall like this the second time? It does so because the ____________________[6] of the coil induced a ____________________[7] in it. This produced a second magnetic field which acted ____________________[8] the movement of the coil and slowed its fall.

6 Draw and label a diagram (or diagrams) of the above experiment.

7 Look for Lenz's Law on the Internet and find applications that use it. Produce a poster with pictures and texts.

DC and AC

1 Read the text and say which type of current is in each copper conductor. Then label the three parts of the traditional light bulb and say if the power source is AC or DC.

When you connect a power source to an electric circuit such as a length of copper wire, the current which flows is either direct current (DC) or alternating current (AC), depending on the source. With DC the electrons in the conductor all travel in the same direction. With AC they just move to and fro. Both DC and AC can power a load, e.g. a light bulb.

When the electrons move in the thin filament of a light bulb, they rub against each other and other atoms and the friction they produce heats up the filament and makes it glow. It makes no difference whether the electrons travel along the conductor or just move to and fro. It's only important that they move.

Before scientists knew about the structure of the atom and the movement of electrons they believed that electric current flowed from the positive to the negative terminal. Today we know that negatively-charged electrons flow towards the protons, which are positive. (See Unit 1 *What is electricity?*) However, current is still defined as a flow of electrically charged particles from the positive to the negative terminal of a voltage source.

Copper conductor 1: ____________

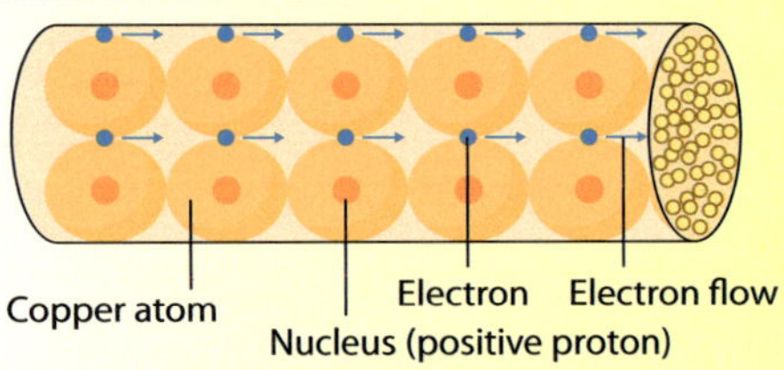

Copper conductor 2: ____________

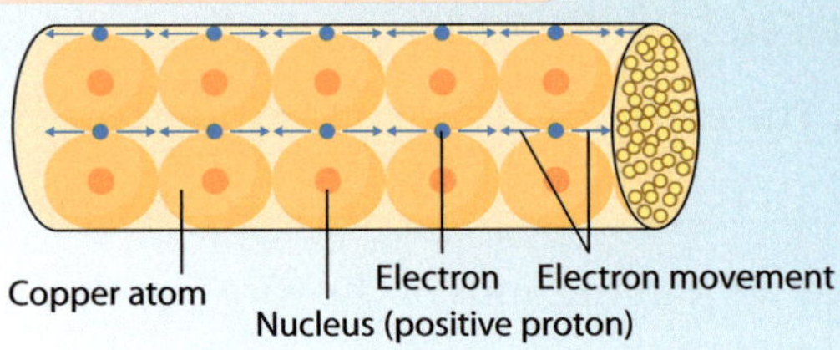

Light bulb: ____________

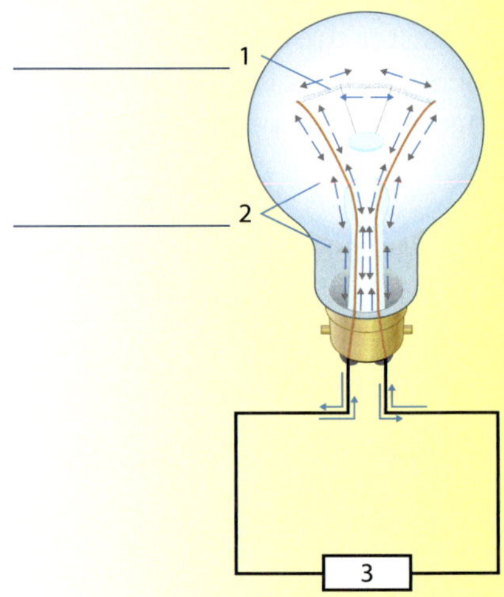

2 Fill in the gaps with words from the text.

If the ______________ 1 in a closed electrical ______________________ 2 flows in one direction only, it is called ________________ 3 current. If the electrons move to and ________________ 4, it is called __________________________ 5 current. In the closed circuit the electrons in the thin ___________________ 6 of a light bulb ___________________ 7 against each other and the light bulb shines brightly. This is because the ___________________________ 8 between the electrons ____________ 9 up the filament and makes it ___________________ 10.

3 Label the devices shown with words from the list and say if they operate on AC or DC.

cordless drill • electric motor • electricity generator • iPod • power drill • shop sign • transformer • video camera

Neon lights and many bigger electric motors use AC, but most electronic devices such as hi-fi and video equipment use DC from (rechargeable) batteries or from an external AC source such as the mains. In this case the AC mains voltage of 230V is first transformed to an acceptable level (e.g. 3 volts) and then rectified to DC.

1
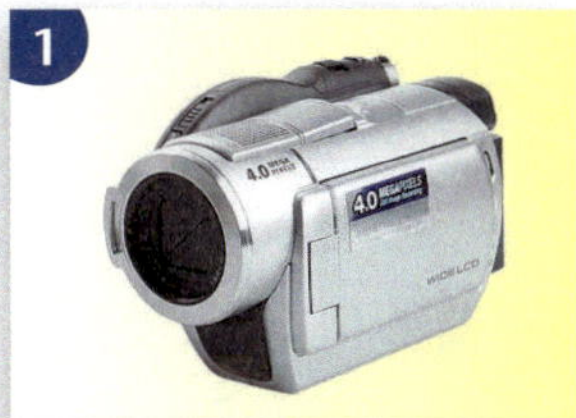

2

3

4
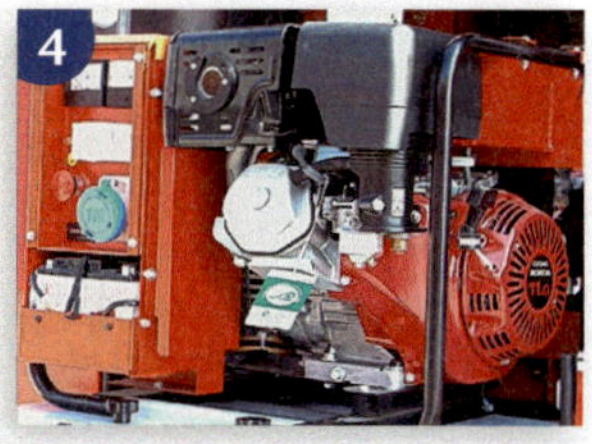

5

6
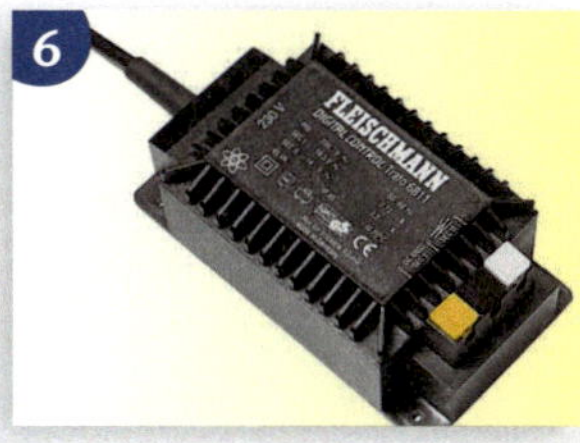

7

8
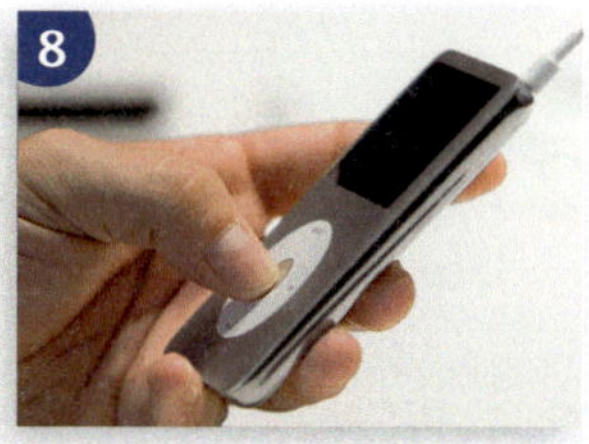

T5 4 Listen to the recording and use the words in the box to label the parts of the drill.

1 ______________________
2 ______________________
3 ______________________
4 ______________________
5 ______________________
6 ______________________
7 ______________________
8 ______________________

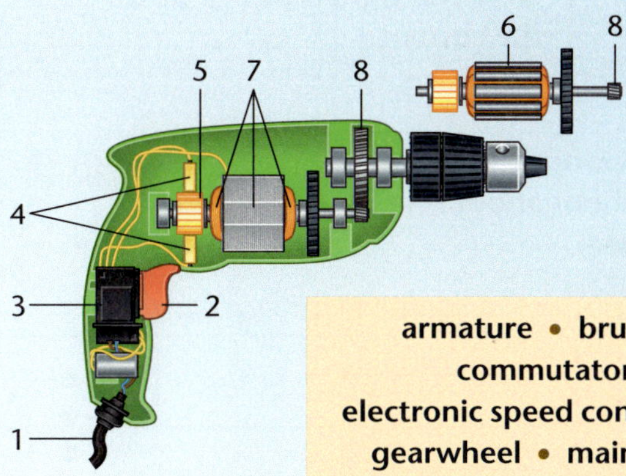

armature • brushes • commutator • electronic speed control unit • gearwheel • mains lead • push button switch • stator

5 Presenting a power tool

With a partner, prepare a short presentation of how another power tool works (e.g. an angle grinder, a belt sander, an electric jigsaw) and give it to the class.

Electrical circuits

1 Name the symbols of components.

antenna • capacitor • coil • crystal earpiece • diode • ground (earth) connection • LED • resistor • switch • variable capacitor

A
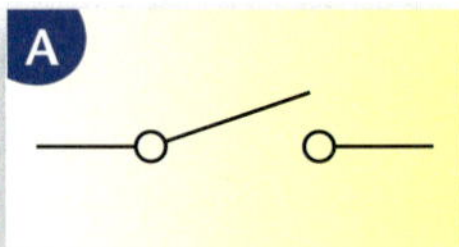

B
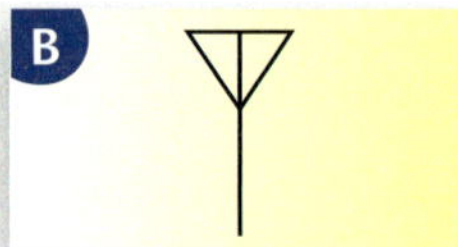

C
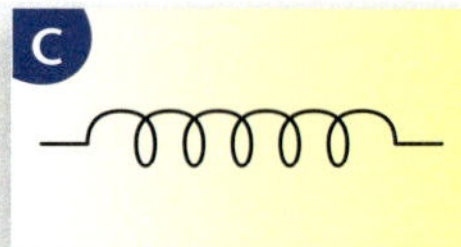

D
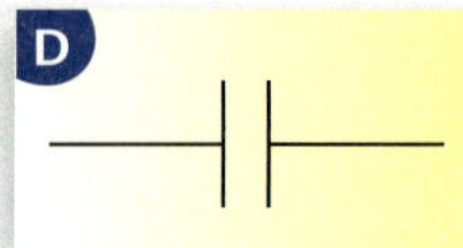

E
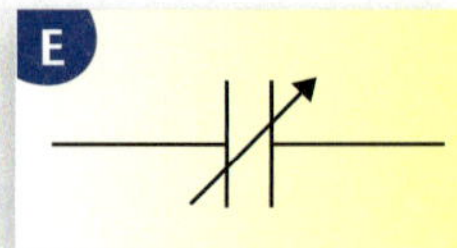

F
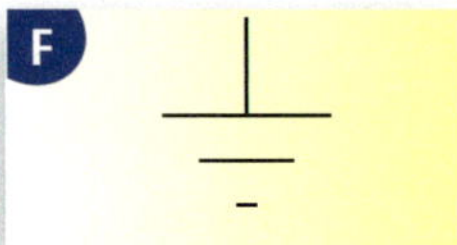

G
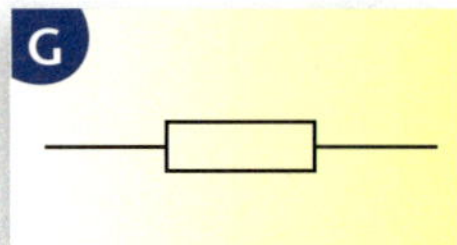

H
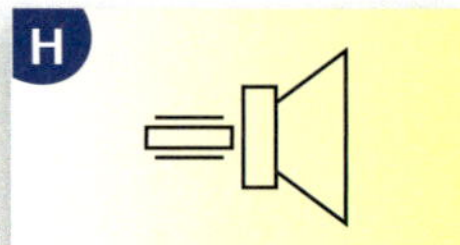

I
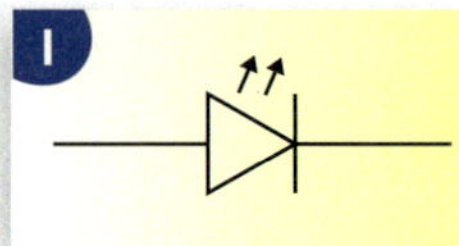

J
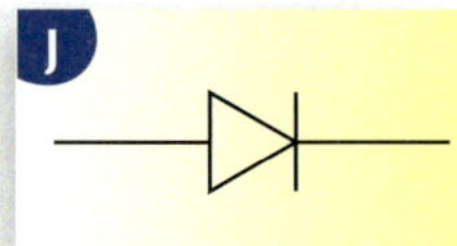

2 A quiz: Form a group and ask each other about the components above. Use the switchboard for your answers.

It	breaks changes leads lowers produces receives or transmits rectifies stores	to earth. light. the circuit. a magnetic field. the voltage. the electrical charge stored. an electric charge. radio signals. electrical signals into sounds. the current.

What does an antenna do in a circuit?

It receives or transmits …

What does …?

3 Work with a partner. Ask and answer questions about this circuit diagram.

What's the component in square **J4** called and what does it do?
– It's a … and it …

Circuit 1

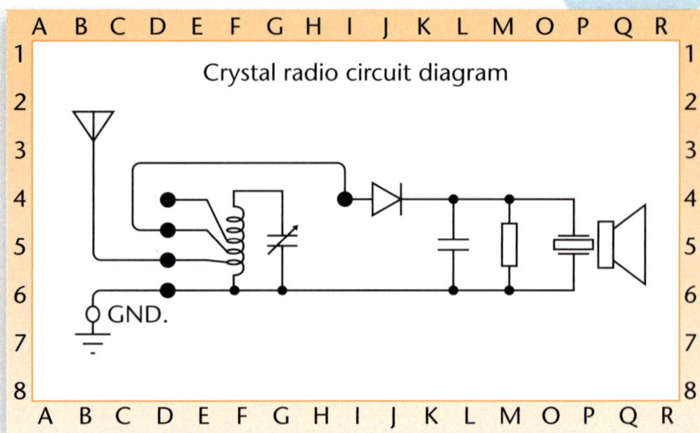

4 Use this example and the language box to write descriptions of circuits 1 and 2.

This circuit consists of four resistors connected to a battery with a switch to turn the circuit on and off. Resistors R_1 and R_2 are alongside each other, so they are in parallel. Resistors R_3 and R_4 are after each other, so they are in series. Currents I_1 and I_2 are different from current I_{Total}. Voltage V_1 is different from V_2. There is an ammeter in the circuit between the switch and the resistors and the two voltmeters show the voltages across R_3 and R_4.

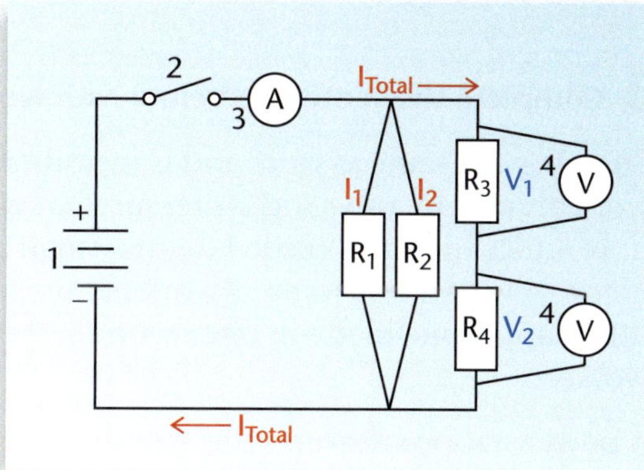

Circuit 2

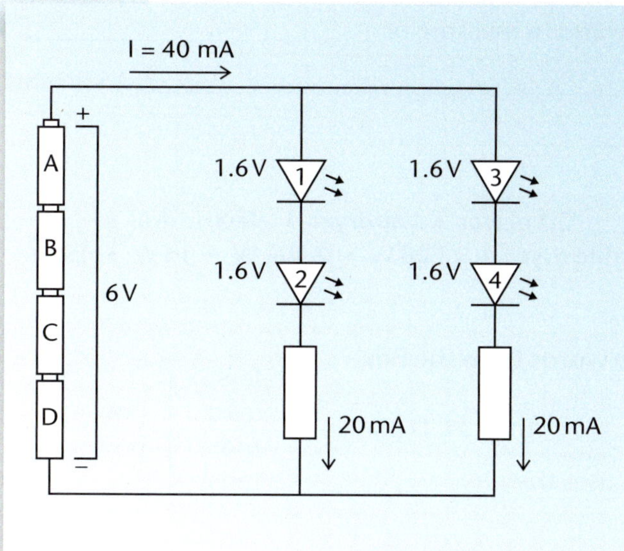

Language box

Circuit 1/2 consists of …
is/are connected to
is/are attached to
travels through
passes through
across/between/alongside
is powered by
is higher/lower than
stays the same
changes the … into …
electrical signals
sounds

5 A teacher is talking to some students. Listen and label the components in the circuit diagram below. The language box can help you.

T6

A simple alarm

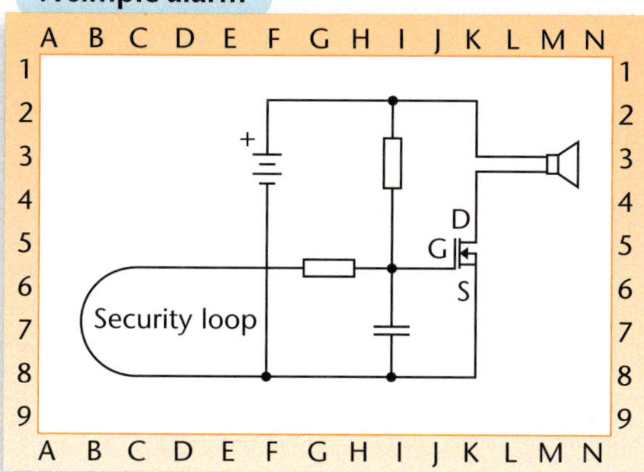

Language box

We write:	We say:
Ω	ohm
0	zero
1.5	one point five
1.55	one point five five
10K	ten K
µF	microfarad

An example of a component number:

BUK456 B – U – K four five six

Electric power

1 Complete the sentences below with words from the text.

Energy is the same as work and is measured in joules. Power is work divided by time and is measured in watts. A joule is about how much energy is needed to lift a small apple (102 g) one metre. A watt is one joule of work per second. Therefore, if you lift an apple one metre in one second, you've done one watt of work.

A power station measures the electricity it supplies to a consumer in kilowatt hours (kWh). One kilowatt is one thousand watts and one hour is 3,600 seconds. One kilowatt hour is therefore 3,600,000 watts per second of work and costs about 30 cents. It would therefore only cost 30 cents to lift 3.6 million apples one metre. Would you do this for 30 cents?

A joule is a measure of ____________ [1]. A watt is a measure of ____________ [2].

Electricity consumption is measured in ____________ [3]. A kilowatt is ____________ [4].

2 Power consumption: Match the appliances with the normal wattages.

CD player • hairdryer • electric drill • tumble dryer • 1,600 W • 2,400 W • 14 W • 450 W

3 Complete the following sentences with two words from the box.

less	
least	powerful
more	power
most	

1 A hairdryer uses ____________ than a CD player.

2 Of all the appliances here, the tumble dryer uses the ____________ ____________ .

3 A CD player is ____________ than an electric drill.

4 The CD player is the ____________ of all the four appliances

5 An electric drill is ____________ than a CD player but ____________ than a tumble dryer.

Mathematical signs

=	equals
+	plus
–	minus
×	times
÷	divided by
≈	about/approximately equal to
4^2	four squared
$\sqrt{16}$	the square root of sixteen
1.4	one point four

Language tips:

- In English, long numbers are separated either by commas or with spaces: 2,840,782 or 2 840 782
- a 60W bulb = a sixty-watt bulb (Here, "watt" is an **adjective**, so there is no plural.)
- The bulb was 60 watts. (Here, "watt" is a **noun**, so there is a plural.)

4 Match each sentence (a-f) with an Ohm's Law equation (1–12).

a) Voltage equals current times resistance. ______

b) Power equals current squared times resistance. ______

c) Voltage equals the square root of power times resistance. ______

d) Resistance equals voltage squared over power. ______

e) Power equals voltage squared divided by resistance. ______

f) Current equals voltage over resistance. ______

Ohm's Law equations

Current (I)

① $\frac{E}{R}$ ② $\frac{P}{E}$ ③ $\frac{\sqrt{P}}{R}$

Resistance (R)

④ $\frac{E}{I}$ ⑤ $\frac{E^2}{P}$ ⑥ $\frac{P}{I^2}$

Voltage (E)

⑦ $I \times R$ ⑧ $\frac{P}{I}$ ⑨ $\sqrt{P \times R}$

Power (P)

⑩ $E \times I$ ⑪ $I^2 \times R$ ⑫ $\frac{E^2}{R}$

5 Complete the sentences with expressions from the exercise above.

1 Power equals voltage ______________________ current.

2 Resistance equals voltage ______________________ current.

3 Current equals ______________________ power over resistance.

4 Voltage equals power ______________________ current.

Did you know..?

In German U stands for voltage. In English it can be E or V.

T7 6 Listen to the two dialogues, make notes below and then write very short summaries in an exercise book and work out the values using a suitable Ohm's Law equation.

1 A customer in an electronics shop has a problem: ______________________

____

Equation: ______________________.

2 Emily Jones is calling an electrical contractor: ______________________

____

Equation: ______________________.

Power distribution

1 Label the diagrams with the highlighted words and numbers from the text.

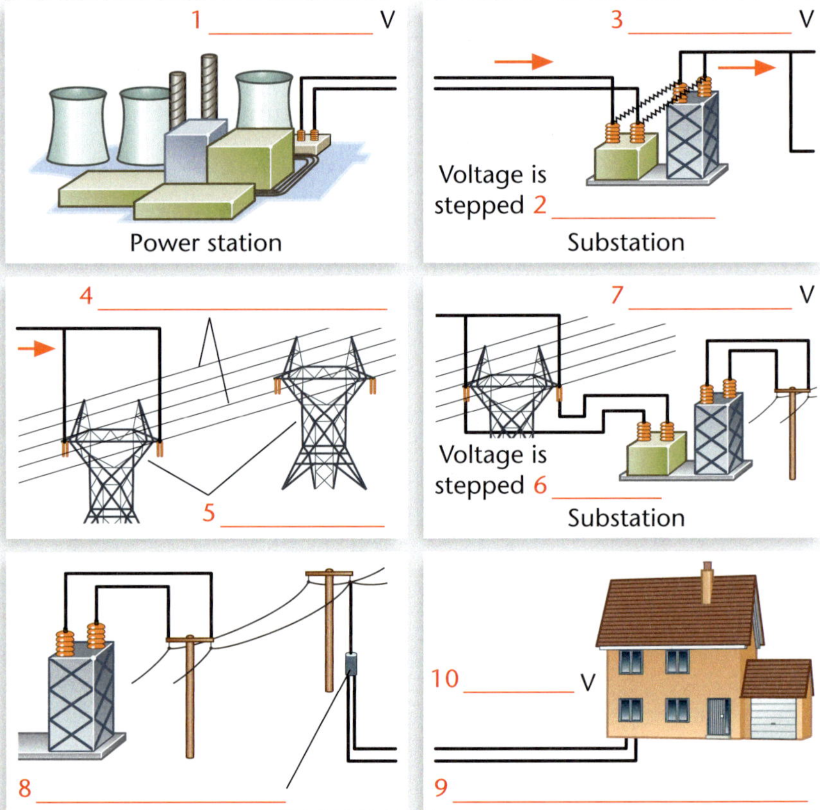

Power stations generate alternating current because it is easier to transmit over long distances. The electricity leaves the station at about **25,000V** and it is then stepped **up** to **380,000V** by transformers at electrical substations. It then travels overland through overhead **high-tension cables** on **pylons** until it reaches its destination. There it is stepped **down** to about **20,000V** at other substations and sent along overhead or **underground cables** to near where it is needed. Step-down transformers are then used to reduce the final voltage to **230V** or **400V** for the consumer.

2 Fill in the gaps with a simple past form from the list. In your exercise book write out the infinitive for each simple past form.

arrested • damaged • hit • made • overloaded • reduced • started • took • was • were

At 8.37 pm on July 13, 1977 lightning ______________ [1] a substation near New York City. A second strike eight minutes later badly ______________ [2] two 345 kV transmission lines. A third strike at 8.55 pm ______________ [3] two more lines fail and this ______________ [4] the whole grid. The power company then ______________ [5] the voltage by 8% but this ______________ [6] not enough. A chain reaction ______________ [7] and at 9.27 pm, just 50 minutes after the first lightning strike, New Yorkers ______________ [8] without electricity. It ______________ [9] almost another 24 hours to get the power back and that night the police ______________ [10] 4,500 looters.

3 Would they work in a blackout? Match the pictures with the words in the list and then use the switchboard to explain what would happen.

calculator • cooker • electrocardiograph • fridge • lamp • laptop computer • lift • mobile phone • traffic lights • TV

1 ______________

2 ______________

3 ______________

4 ______________

5 ______________

6 ______________

7 ______________

8 ______________

9 ______________

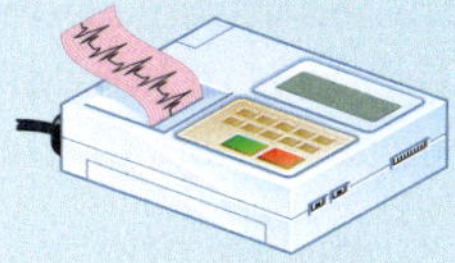

10 ______________

In a blackout the ...	would	work because it	runs	off the mains.
	wouldn't		doesn't run	a 230V power supply.
			needs	a 60 V power supply.
			doesn't need	on batteries.
			has	its own power supply.
			doesn't have	rechargeable.
			is	electricity all the time.
			isn't	

T8

4 Listen to the dialogue between an old lady and her electricity supplier and complete the sentences below. The words in the box can help you.

a circuit-breaker
to disconnect
some toast
the consumer unit
the fuse box
a power cut
to plug in
to short-circuit
metal knife
a technician

1 Doris wants to speak to a ______________________________.

2 She thinks there has been a ______________________________.

3 Doris has never heard of ______________________________.

4 Older people call it the ______________________________.

5 The lights went off when she was making ______________________________.

6 When Doris used the metal knife she ______________________________.

7 The technician first tells Doris to ______________________________.

8 Then he tells her to check ______________________________.

9 Finally, he tells her to ______________________________.

10 He advises her never to ______________________________.

Storing electrical energy

1 Complete the sentences with words from the text.

If you only need a small amount of electrical energy over a period of time for a device such as a torch or a mobile phone, a rechargeable or non-rechargeable battery is enough. However, if you need a small amount of power very quickly, you need a capacitor. Capacitors don't generate electricity with a chemical reaction like a battery. They only store electrons and can release them in a fraction of a second, which means that they can also be very dangerous. A camera flash unit, for example, has a capacitor. Capacitors can also be recharged in a few seconds and used over and over again and nowadays so-called supercapacitors even power electric buses. They run without overhead power lines and are quickly recharged each time they stop. Storing power for the power grid is a very different problem because of the huge quantities of energy needed. One answer is a pumped storage power plant using water (e.g. in Goldisthal, Thuringia), which can store thousands of kilowatts of off-peak electricity for later use. Another solution is a compressed air energy storage plant such as the Iowa Stored Energy Plant in the USA.

1 A mobile phone uses a …
2 Capacitors deliver power …
3 A capacitor doesn't …
4 Capacitors can be dangerous because …
5 You can recharge a capacitor in …
6 Buses with supercapacitors don't need …
7 Huge quantities of energy are needed for …
8 Large quantities of power can be stored at …

2 Use words from the diagram to fill in the gaps in the text.

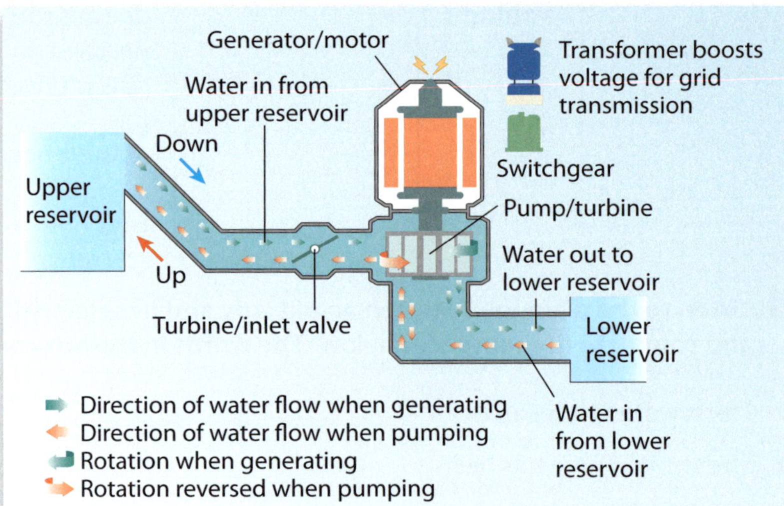

Pumped storage power plant

A pumped ________________ [1] power plant is one of the most efficient ways of storing a very large quantity of power. Water is pumped from a lower to an upper ____________ [2] with an electric ___________ [3] which drives a ___________ [4] at times when there is extra power. On its way ________________________________ [5] the water passes through an __________________ ____________________ [6] and is stored until needed. Later, when more electricity is needed it flows ____________ [7] to the lower level and spins a __________________ [8] which generates electricity. The electricity generated first goes through a ___________________ [9] unit and is then stepped up to a much higher ______________ [10] by a ___________________ [11] before it enters the power _______________________ [12].

3 Label the pictures and then translate them into German. Can you think of other devices powered by capacitors? Make a list in your exercise book.

fork-lift truck • MRI scanner • plasma TV • X-ray machine

1 ________________

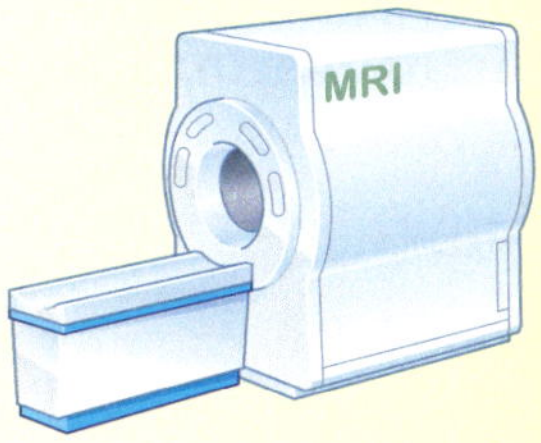

2 ________________

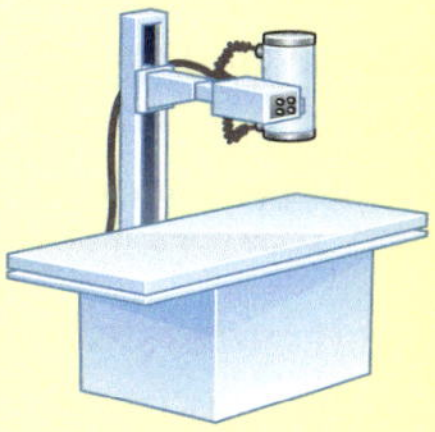

3 ________________

4 ________________

4 When is it cool to buy a new fridge? Study the table and the US government's EnergyGuide label on all new fridges and then fill in the gaps.

If your fridge was made before / between / after	it uses about this much energy per year.	Replacing it with an energy-efficient model will save about
<1976	1800 kWh	$151 per year
1976-86	1400 kWh	$107 per year
1987-89	950 kWh	$58 per year
1990-92	900 kWh	$52 per year
1993-00	700 kWh	$30 per year
2001+	500 kWh	$8 per year

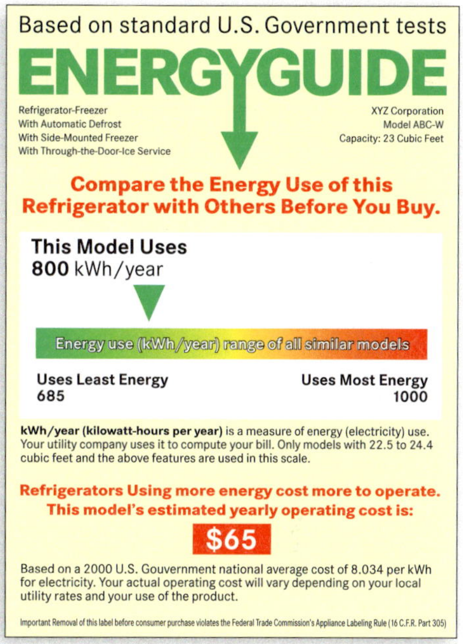
Based on standard U.S. Government tests

ENERGYGUIDE

Refrigerator-Freezer
With Automatic Defrost
With Side-Mounted Freezer
With Through-the-Door-Ice Service

XYZ Corporation
Model ABC-W
Capacity: 23 Cubic Feet

Compare the Energy Use of this Refrigerator with Others Before You Buy.

This Model Uses
800 kWh/year

Energy use (kWh/year) range of all similar models

Uses Least Energy
685

Uses Most Energy
1000

kWh/year (kilowatt-hours per year) is a measure of energy (electricity) use. Your utility company uses it to compute your bill. Only models with 22.5 to 24.4 cubic feet and the above features are used in this scale.

Refrigerators Using more energy cost more to operate. This model's estimated yearly operating cost is:

$65

Based on a 2000 U.S. Gouvernment national average cost of 8.034 per kWh for electricity. Your actual operating cost will vary depending on your local utility rates and your use of the product.

Important Removal of this label before consumer purchase violates the Federal Trade Commission's Appliance Labeling Rule (16 C.F.R. Part 305)

Large fridges made ________ 1 1976 use about __________ 2 of electricity per year. If you replace a very old fridge with a new ____________________ 3 model you can save about ______________ 4 per year. The EnergyGuide label here shows that the fridge in question uses ______________ 5 of electricity and costs ____________________ 6 to operate per year. The table shows that a fridge made between ______________ 7 and ________________ 8 only uses half as much electricity as one made before 1976. If your fridge was made after ______________ 9 it will use only about 500 ____________ 10 of electricity per year so you'll only save about ______________ 11 per year if you buy a new one.

5 Project

Look at the specification plates on your fridge/electric cooker/dishwasher/washing machine/ computer/stereo and work out how much power it costs to operate them at maximum performance for 1 hour. Next work out how much they cost to run for a year. Find out the price of 1 kWh from your energy supplier or assume it's 0.1535 €/kWh. Use a watt-hour meter (power measuring meter) if you have one. Present your results to the class with a partner.

Safety devices

1 Use words from the text to name the safety devices.

Electrical engineers make sure a circuit has a weak point which breaks first if it is overloaded. This stops the circuit from overheating, catching fire, damaging equipment and harming people.

There are three types of safety devices in electrical circuits:

A fuse – it blows. This means it breaks when overloaded. You can't reset it, so you replace the whole fuse, e.g. a blade fuse in a car or a cartridge fuse in an electrical device or the wire in a rewirable fuse* because it burns through. Fuses are cheap.

A circuit breaker – It trips when overloaded and can be reset. It protects electrical appliances, e.g. a toaster or a washing machine but doesn't protect people because it lets a lot of current through, e.g. 16A, before it trips. Circuit breakers are expensive.

An RCD (residual current device) – It trips when overloaded and can be reset. It is highly sensitive and trips if there's a faulty current of as little as 30 mA. Its job is to protect people and it is used e.g. in bathrooms and for outside devices, e.g. the socket for a hedge trimmer. RCDs are expensive.

1
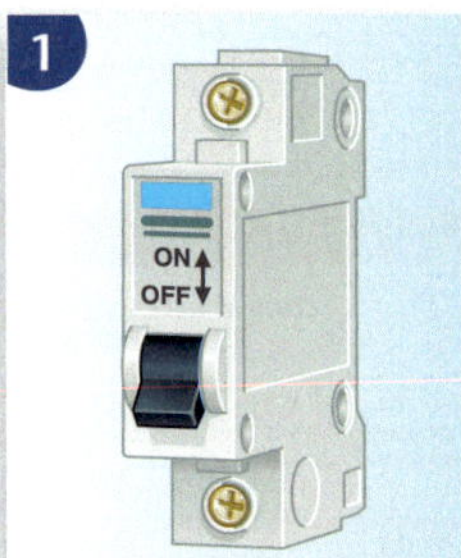

2
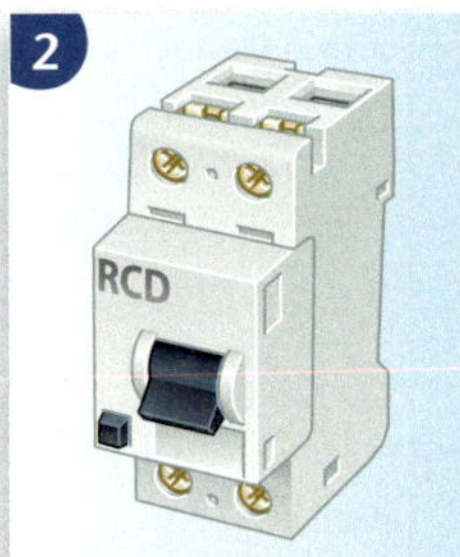

3
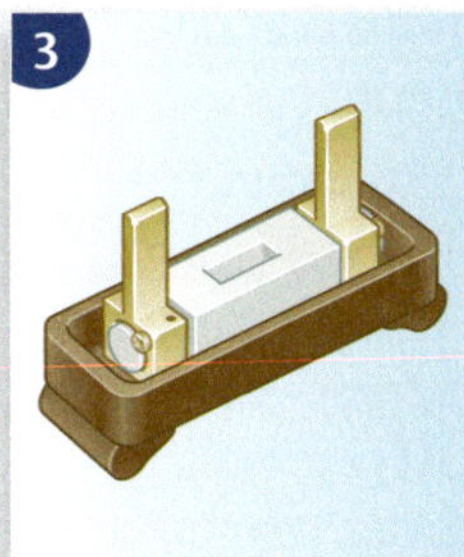

4
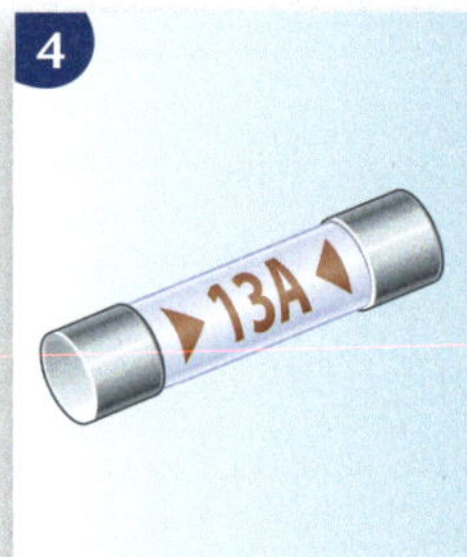

5
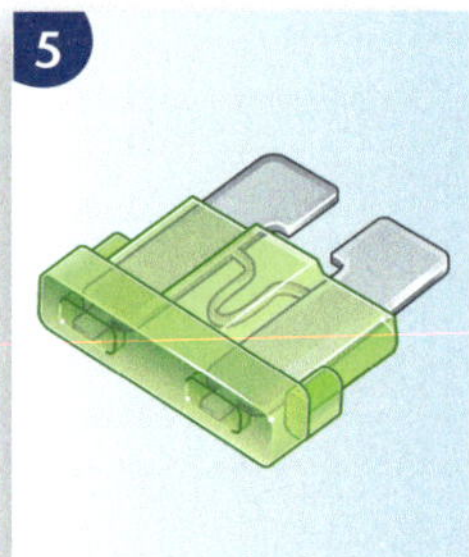

(* used only in UK)

2 Match the sentence halves.

1	A fuse is the part of the circuit	**A**	protects people.
2	A fuse can't	**B**	it trips.
3	When a fuse is overloaded	**C**	more than a fuse.
4	Circuit breakers	**D**	which breaks first.
5	A circuit breaker costs	**E**	will trip an RCD.
6	When a circuit breaker is overloaded	**F**	can be reset.
7	An RCD	**G**	be reset.
8	A very small faulty current	**H**	it blows.

3 That's not how we do it over here! Study the text and the diagram and then compare the British and the German household wiring systems.

In many houses in Britain there are basically two circuits – a 30 amp ring circuit to power electrical equipment (e.g. a dishwasher) and a 5 amp lighting circuit. Some appliances also have their own circuit or are connected to an existing circuit with a spur and a switched fused connection unit (e.g. for an electric shower). Each circuit has a circuit breaker in the consumer unit. In addition to this, British plugs have a 3, 5 or 13 amp cartridge fuse which blows if overloaded.

Safety devices in household wiring

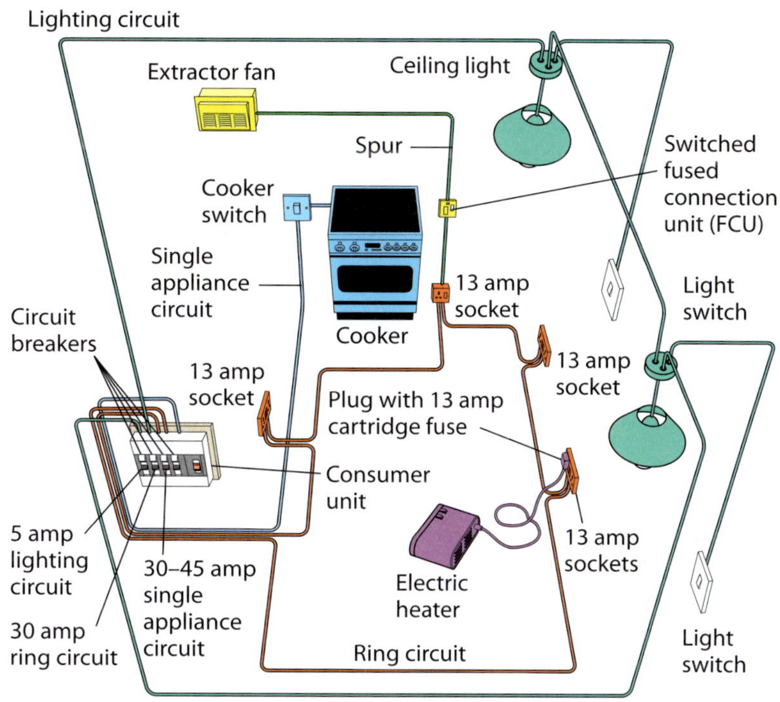

In British/German houses	there is/isn't	a circuit breaker for …
A British/German electrician	there are/aren't	only two circuits.
In Britain/Germany, appliances	uses	a … amp …
A British/German plug	doesn't use	… amp circuit breakers.
…	has	a separate switch for the …
	doesn't have	one big circuit breaker for …
	have	…
	don't have	…

T9

4 Sebastian Fischer is a German electrician on work placement in Britain. Today he's looking at the wiring in an old pub. Listen to the dialogue and then complete the following tasks.

1 Make a list of all the things that surprise him.

2 Say what you or your company would do to solve the problem in the pub.

Giving a presentation

- This diagram shows how …
- Here we can see …
- The purpose of an RCD/a fuse/… is to protect appliances/prevent fires/…
- Each circuit has/contains …
- If the fuse blows/the circuit breaker trips, it can/can't be reset/replaced/…
- If there is a faulty current, …

5 Presentation

Draw a circuit diagram of the wiring in your own flat or house (or part of it) and then give a presentation to the class explaining what safety features it has and how they work.

Safety rules

5 SICHERHEITSREGELN

Vor Beginn der Arbeiten
- **Freischalten**
- **Gegen Wiedereinschalten sichern**
- **Spannungsfreiheit feststellen**
- **Erden und kurzschließen**
- **Benachbarte, unter Spannung stehende Teile abdecken oder abschranken**

1 How good is your English? Choose the statements which correctly explain each of the five safety rules in German.

Rule no. 1: Before you work on electrical equipment or a circuit or you must
- **a** switch it off.
- **b** turn it off.
- **c** disconnect it.

Rule no. 2: The next thing you must do is
- **a** tell your workmates that you're working on the circuit or equipment.
- **b** lock and tag it so no one turns it back on again.
- **c** test the circuit to see if it's still live.

Rule no. 3: If, for example, the multimeter reading for the circuit is zero
- **a** you still mustn't start work on it.
- **b** it's safe to start work on it.
- **c** you can be sure the circuit isn't live.

Rule no. 4: You short-circuit a circuit by
- **a** touching the black conductor against the blue conductor.
- **b** touching the blue conductor against the green-yellow conductor.
- **c** touching the black conductor against the green-yellow conductor.

Rule no. 5: If there are live electrical components near where you're working
- **a** don't start work until you've disconnected them.
- **b** make it impossible to touch them if you can't disconnect them.
- **c** be careful not to touch them.

2 Match the explanations with the signs.

- **A** This equipment will not stop electrical equipment or installations from burning.
- **B** There is no insulation on these conductors. If you touch them you will get a shock.
- **C** You mustn't block this door because someone might need to open it quickly.
- **D** Electricity enters this building underground, so you must be careful when using earth-moving machinery or tools.
- **E** You mustn't switch this circuit back on again. Only the person who switched it off is allowed to switch it back on again.

Make a list of the signs you see at your workplace and explain them in English.

1 

___

2 

___

3 

___

4 

___

5 

___

3 Use the language box to fill in the gaps.

Only a qualified electrician ______________________ [1] do electrical installation work. If you aren't a qualified electrician you ______________________ [2] work on a circuit. Even when you're qualified you ______________________ [3] always read the safety warningsbefore starting work. You also ______________________ [4] forget to switch off the circuit breaker and put a sign on the consumer unit. If you see a label on a circuit to say that another person has locked it out, you ______________________ [5] switch it back on again. You ______________________ [6] wait for that person to do so.

Language box

must	müssen
am/is/are allowed to	dürfen
mustn't	darf/soll nicht
am not/isn't/aren't allowed to	darf nicht

4 Interpreting for an English-speaking colleague

You are an apprentice electrician at Elektro Klein and today you have a British trainee called Alan Turner with you. You're about to work on an electrical circuit. Before you start, explain to Alan what your foreman says about the safety rules. Work with two partners and role play the dialogue.
Use expressions like "He says that / He wants to know if…". (*überprüfen/kontrollieren = check*)

Elektromeister	You	Alan
1. Was müsst ihr zuerst überprüfen, bevor ihr anfangt?	2. *He wants to know what ...*	3. We should check to see if the circuit is live.
	4. …	
5. Nicht schlecht, aber nicht richtig!	6. …	7. OK, so what's the first step?
	8. …	
9. Ihr müsst zuerst den Stromkreis freischalten.	10. …	11. Ah yes, of course! Where do we disconnect it – at the consumer unit?
	12. …	
13. Richtig! Könnt ihr jetzt mit der Arbeit anfangen?	14. …	15. I don't think so. I think we should now check to see if the circuit's live.
	16. …	
17. Noch nicht! Als Nächstes müßt ihr ein Schild an den Sicherungskasten hängen, damit niemand den Schaltkreis wieder einschaltet.	18. …	19. Yes, that makes sense. And after you've put the sign on the consumer unit, what's next?

T10 **Now listen to the example dialogue on the CD and check how well you interpreted.**

5 Explain the other safety rules to Alan in English.

Electric lighting

T11 **1 How many of these light sources can you name? How energy-efficient do you think they are? Then listen to the recording and check your answers.**

Light source		Properties	Efficiency
A ________	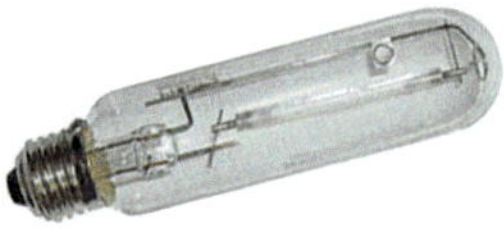	Produces yellow light; extremely energy-efficient; very long life; limited use	____%
B ________	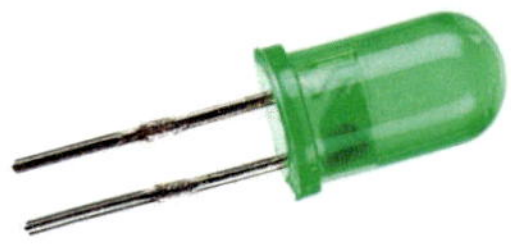	Available in many colours; energy-efficient; doesn't get hot; long life; used in electronic equipment and for decoration; some types are expensive	____%
C ________		Energy-efficient; good colour rendition; contains mercury; expensive; not dimmable	____%
D ________		Energy-efficient; good colour rendition; long life; can produce ultra-violet light for medical and cosmetic use; contains mercury; expensive; not dimmable	____%
E ________	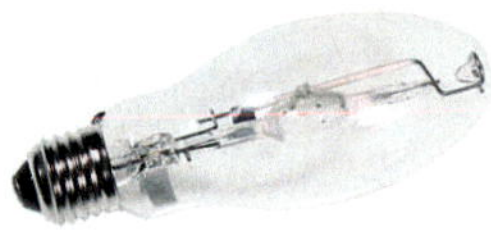	Very powerful light; used for floodlights at sports stadiums; good colour rendition; takes several minutes to warm up or restart; can explode	____%
F ________		Extremely intense light used in film projectors; must be water-cooled; gas is under high pressure; can explode	____%
G ________	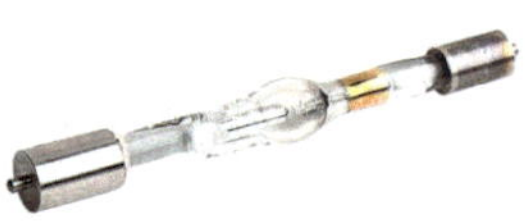	Very bright light; dimmable; can be used inside, outside and in vehicles; can become very hot; bulb blows sooner if touched	____%
H ________		Excellent colour rendition (produces warm, natural light); cheap to replace; dimmable; short life; highly inefficient	____%

2 Select the right light source (A–H) from above for the following uses:

1 an energy-saving ceiling light
2 a strip light for the kitchen
3 decorative lighting in a home
4 a powerful garden light
5 a street light
6 stadium floodlights
7 an old-style outdoor light
8 a film projector

1____ 2____ 3____ 4____ 5____ 6____ 7____ 8____

3 Use the switchboard to write sentences about the eight light sources and their uses.

A …	is/are	used for	projectors	because	it's	safe.
CFLs	is/are often	found in	car headlights		they're	cheap.
LEDs	is/are normally		street lighting			soft.
…	is/are sometimes		floodlights			bright.
			an outdoor light			efficient.
			ceiling lights			attractive.
			decorative lighting			powerful.
			a car dashboard			economical.
			household lighting			expensive.
			…			…

1 *A halogen lamp is used …*

2 *CFLS are …*

3

4

5

6

7

8

4 Complete the sentences with a suitable comparison.

dangerous • efficient • expensive • bright • cheap • soft • long • short

Comparisons

Short adjectives:
short – shorter than – (the) shortest
Long adjectives:
economical – more/less economical than – (the) most/least economical

1 LEDs only cost a few cents so they are ______________________ CFLs.

2 A fluorescent tube is ______________________ a halogen lamp but ______________________ a sodium lamp.

3 Of all the light sources sodium lamps have ______________________ life span.

4 Of all the light sources an incandescent bulb is ______________________ .

5 The pressurized gas in a xenon short arc lamp makes it ______________________ a CFL.

5 An energy survey: With a partner list the sources of electric light in your (a) classroom, (b) own home, and (c) workplace. Give a presentation on what you find and include the following factors:

cost and efficiency • safety • environmental dangers • colour • rendition

Use the following expressions:
We now wish to present you with the results of our energy survey.
We found that…
The following data/chart/graph/diagram shows that…
… is/are often used in the workshop/laboratory/classroom/… because…
It would be better/safer/cheaper/more efficient/less dangerous to … because…
If we changed over to CFLs/…, we would make a saving of …%

DC motors

T12 **1 How to build a DC motor in 10 minutes: Put the instructions (A–J) in the same order as the photos then listen to the recording and check your answer.**

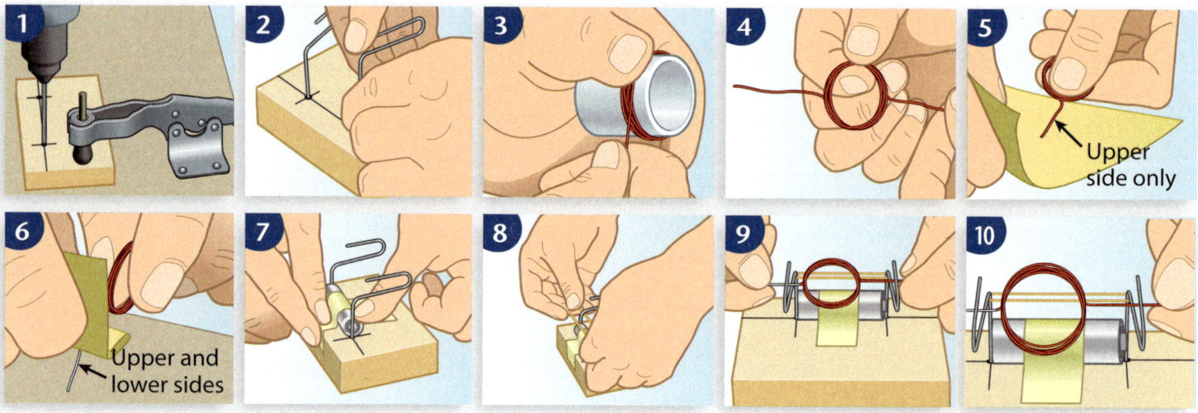

Materials required

- an AA battery
- a rubber band
- two paper clips
- a square magnet
- a piece of plastic tube
- 40 cm of insulated wire
- a piece of fine sandpaper
- a small block of wood

A Bend open the two paper clips to form metal holders and insert them into the holes in the wooden base.
B Completely sand away 5 cm of the insulation from the other end of the wire.
C Drill two holes in the block of wood 5 cm apart (the length of an AA battery).
D Give the top of the coil a gentle push to start it turning. It will then spin alone.
E Leave 5 cm of wire free at each end and wrap the ends of the wire around the coil so they stick out exactly opposite each other.
F Place the rubber band around the paper clip holders so they press hard against the terminals of the battery.
G Place the two ends of the coil in the metal paper clip holders. Place the magnet under the coil.
H Sand away 5 cm of the insulation from the upper side of one end of the wire. The lower side of the wire remains insulated.
I Tape the battery to the wooden base so its ends touch the two paper clips.
J Wrap the wire around the plastic tube seven times to make a coil.

1___ 2___ 3___ 4___ 5___ 6___ 7___ 8___ 9___ 10___

2 Read the text and then label the diagram (1–6) with the highlighted words.

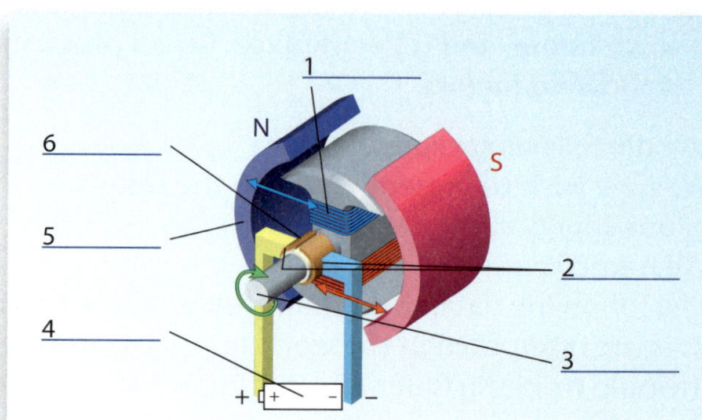

In a DC motor there is a **permanent magnet (stator)** around an **armature**, which is a coil of wire wound around a piece of iron. The armature is mounted on an **axle** so it can turn freely. The magnet doesn't move. The armature is connected to a **battery** by **brushes** which press against one end of it. The current from the battery travels along the coil of wire and produces a magnetic field around the armature. When the north end of this field is next to the north end of the permanent magnet the armature is repelled. The result is the rotation of the armature away from the permanent magnet's magnetic field. At this point the armature would normally stop but it doesn't because the current enters it through the two plates of a **split-ring commutator**. After it has turned 180° the armature changes polarity because the commutator reverses the direction of the current with each half-turn.

3 Complete the sentences with words from the text.

1 A stator is ____.

2 The armature can turn because ____

____.

3 The current reaches the armature through ____.

4 The north end of the permanent magnet repels ____

____.

5 The brushes press against the plates of ____.

6 The function of the commutator is to ____.

4 Use prepositions from the text to fill in the gaps.

If a DC motor only has an armature __________[1] two poles there are only two plates __________[2] the commutator, so when the armature turns __________[3] the axle it comes __________[4] a position where each commutator brush presses __________[5] both commutator plates __________[6] the same time, which produces a short circuit. In order to use the current __________[7] the battery all the time, a DC motor usually has three or more poles. If a motor has a 3-pole armature, one __________[8] its poles will always be repelled __________[9] the stator's magnetic field __________[10] any time, making it run more smoothly.

5 Choose a presentation

- Work with a partner and use the instructions in exercise 1 to make the DC motor described. Bring in the materials and as one of you assembles the motor in front of the class, the other explains each step. Use the expressions in the language box.
- Use the Internet to find more examples of simple DC motors (e.g. with a nail). Find or draw diagrams which show the materials they need and how they are assembled. Present them to the class, explaining each step as you go.

First ..., Then ..., Next ...,
After that ..., Finally ...
You make sure that ...
For this motor you'll need ...
Take the ... and bend/cut/... it.
You use the tube/the sandpaper to ...
You have to do this because...
Carefully, slowly, gently
You can see that ...
This is because ...

3-phase induction motor

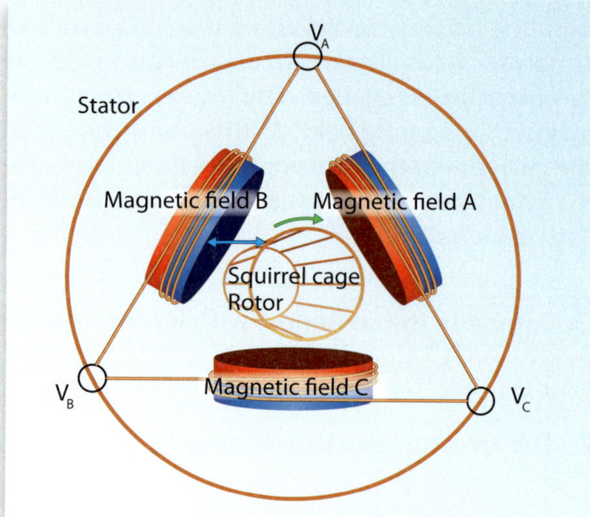

1 Read the text and look at the diagram to match the sentence halves.

A 3-phase induction motor has a stator in which there is a rotating magnetic field around a rotor. The rotating magnetic field in the stator induces a current in the copper rods of the rotor. This current generates a second magnetic field around the rotor. In the diagram the north polarity of the rotor is repelled by the north polarity of magnetic field B so the rotor turns away from it. At the same time the north polarity of the rotor is attracted by the south polarity of magnetic field A, so it turns towards it. This happens again and again as the rotor moves through the magnetic fields. Magnetic fields A, B and C are produced by the three phases of the AC mains supply, which in Europe has a frequency of 50 Hertz, meaning it changes polarity 50 times per second. The speed at which the rotor turns is controlled by the number of magnetic fields in the stator and the frequency of the AC supply voltage, so a 3-phase induction motor will naturally reach one speed and stay at that speed. In the past this was a major disadvantage but nowadays it is possible to use an electronic variable frequency drive (VFD) to regulate how often the magnetic fields change polarity and therefore the speed at which the rotor turns.

1 There is a rotating magnetic field
2 The rotor is made of
3 A second magnetic field is generated
4 The north polarity in the stator
5 50 hertz means that every second
6 How fast the rotor turns depends
7 Nowadays it's easier to
8 A VFD regulates how often

A the mains supply changes polarity fifty times
B the AC mains supply changes polarity
C control the speed of the motor
D on two factors
E around the rotor
F in the stator
G copper rods
H repels the north polarity in the rotor

1 ____ 2 ____ 3 ____ 4 ____ 5 ____ 6 ____ 7 ____ 8 ____

2 Use words from the text to fill in the crossword.

Across

4 The alternating current in this motor has three … .
6 The opposite of 'repel' is … .
7 The magnetic … in the stator produces another one in the rotor.
8 The rotor is made of … .
10 The short form of 'alternating current' is … .
11 The … is the part of the motor which doesn't move.
12 A magnetic field which turns is a … magnetic field.

Down

1 The opposite of 'attract' is …
2 In Europe alternating current has a … of 50 hertz.
3 Something which you can change is … .
5 Frequency is measured in … .
9 If a magnetic field changes from north to south, it changes … .

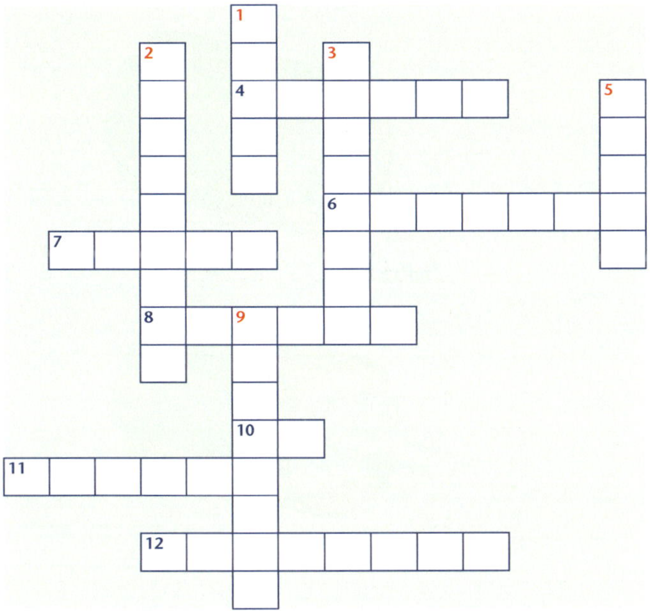

The 'Hertz' is named after the German physicist Heinrich Rudolf Hertz . He was born in Hamburg on February 22, 1857. He died in Bonn on January 1, 1894, aged 36.

3 Fill in the gaps with words from the recording.

T 13 **Jenny Green's company has just bought an office block in Berlin. The building is over 50 years old and the ventilation system is inefficient, so Jenny has asked Andreas Ritter from Horstmeier Luft- und Klimatechnik GmbH to give her some advice.**

1 Jenny and Andreas are on the ______________ of the building.

2 The ventilation system is just a big air shaft with a ______________ on it.

3 Andreas suggests installing a supply and a return ______________ .

4 One will suck in fresh air and the other will ______________ stale air.

5 The motors will be AC ______________ motors.

6 By using a VFD you can ______________ the speed of the motor.

7 A VFD is ______________ - free.

8 The part of the motor which moves is the ______________ - cage rotor.

9 Torque is the ______________ you need to turn something.

10 Andreas will send Jenny an ______________ in the next few days.

4 AC or DC motor? Write the correct motor type for each application. Then list 6 more examples.

1. electric car: ____ **2.** washing-machine: ____ **3.** electric car aerial: ____

4. cordless drill: ____ **5.** electric water pump: ____ **6.** electric fan: ____

7. car seat-positioning motor: ____ **8.** compressor: ____ **9.** lift: ____

10. ______________: ____ **11.** ______________: ____ **12.** ______________: ____

13. ______________: ____ **14.** ______________: ____ **15.** ______________: ____

Pure electric vehicles

1 Read the text, label the diagram with the highlighted words. Say which motors are AC and DC.

EVs use different types of electric motors, depending on the jobs they must do. The oldest motor type is a DC motor with **brushes**. These have a **permanent magnet** around a rotating **armature** with windings. The armature is connected to a **commutator**. DC motors can also be brushless and in such motors a **permanent magnet** rotates inside **field coils** on the outside of the motor. An **encoder** on the axle of the permanent magnet controls when the field magnets change polarity. In AC induction motors there is often a **squirrel-cage rotor** made of **windings** or copper rods inside a stator with a **rotating magnetic field**.

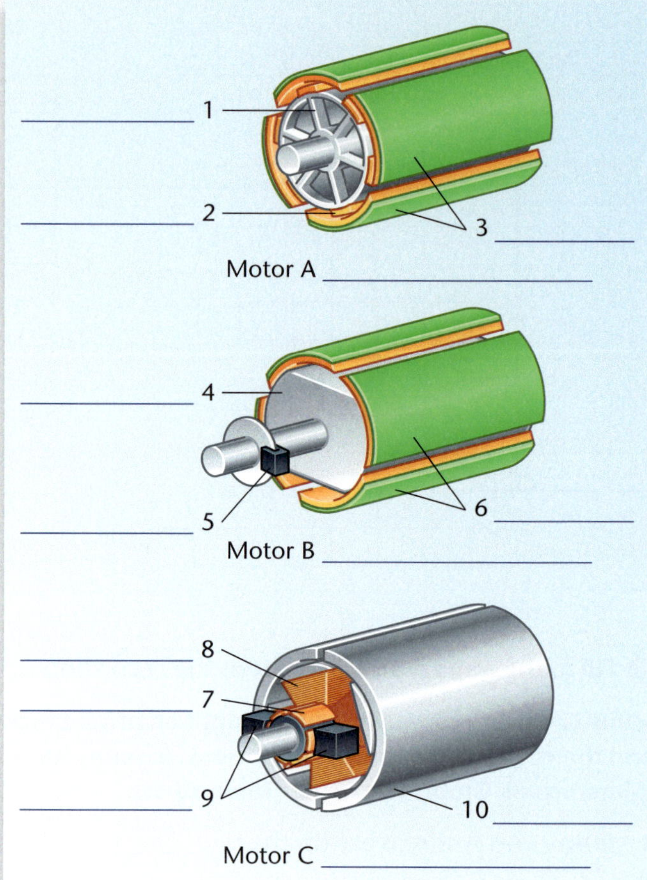

2 Use the dialogue to reply to the statements after it.

T14 Jane Riley is a reporter for *Top Gear*, a radio programme about trends in the car industry. Listen to her talking to Tom Bell, whose company makes electric cars.

Jane Hello and welcome to *Top Gear*. Today I'm talking to Tom Bell about EVs and if you're not quite sure what that means, an EV is an electric vehicle. Why should I buy an EV, Tom?

Tom There are so many reasons I just don't know where to start, so I suggest you come for a test drive in one of our electric sports cars. We can talk while we're driving.

Jane Won't it be too noisy?

Tom Let's find out, shall we? Here's the car. Would you like to get in? Please fasten your seat belt. And off we go!

Jane Wow, it's really fast! It's like a Formula 1 racing car!

Tom That's right. It accelerates from nought to 60 miles per hour in just four seconds. And did you hear any noise?

Jane There was none at all! It's like a ghost!

Tom Exactly. This is a pure electric car. It's so quiet that you can drive it at night without waking people up and it also has zero emissions.

Jane That's great news for the environment, Tom, but how come it's so fast?

Tom Electric motors have very high power even at low speeds, which means you can accelerate very quickly. This car will actually do 125 mph. And you don't need to change gear in this vehicle because there's no gearbox. It drives like an automatic.

Jane Well that certainly does make things a lot easier! Now where does all this power come from?

Tom It's from the lithium-ion battery pack behind our seats. Let's just stop here and I'll show you. Let's get out and look at the back of the car. You just plug the power cord into this socket here to recharge the batteries.

Jane But where can you recharge them and how long does it take? You can't just go to a petrol station, can you?

Tom Not yet, but you soon will! When you buy this car you get a home charging station, which we install in your garage, so you can recharge the batteries in three and a half hours. Most people do this overnight. And soon there'll be a network of charging stations all over the country. There's just one more thing I think I should tell your listeners, Jane. This car has regenerative braking, which means that when it slows down the motor actually recharges the battery, so it's about 90% efficient.

Jane This is very clever stuff! And what about the range?

Tom It has a range of 200 miles, which is about 320 km, per battery charge.

Jane And the price?

Tom About $100,000, which is what you'd pay for a Porsche or a BMW.

1. EVs are slow! – No, they aren't! They …
2. Cars are noisy and pollute the environment! – EVs aren't! They're …
3. EVs are hard to drive! – …
4. The battery takes all night to recharge! – …
5. Cars waste energy! – …
6. EVs have a very short range! – …

3 Write a dialogue in which you help a customer talk to a salesman selling EVs at a car show.

Kunde/-in	Verkäufer/-in
1. Sie fragen die/den Verkäufer/-in, ob das ein Elektroauto ist.	**2.** Ja, das stimmt! Es ist ein rein elektrisch betriebenes Fahrzeug und hat Lithium-Ionen-Batterien.
3. Sie haben gehört, dass elektrische Fahrzeuge langsam sind.	**4.** Sie waren langsam aber jetzt sind sie viel schneller.
5. Wie ist die Beschleunigung?	**6.** Dieser Sportwagen beschleunigt auf Tempo 100 in 4 Sekunden.
7. Das ist sehr schnell! Stimmt es, dass man die Batterien jeden Tag über Nacht aufladen muss?	**8.** Das stimmt nicht! Man hat eine Reichweite von 320 km pro Ladung, also kann man lange fahren, ohne die Batterien aufzuladen.
9. Wie ist die Batterieladezeit?	**10.** Man braucht dreieinhalb Stunden, um die Batterien aufzuladen.
11. Wo kann man die Batterie aufladen?	**12.** Wenn man dieses Fahrzeug kauft, bekommt man auch eine Ladestation für zu Hause, aber bald wird es ein Netz von Ladestationen geben.
13. Sie bedanken sich für die Informationen.	**14.** Gern geschehen!

Hybrid vehicles

1 Read the text and label the diagrams with the condition they show.

A hybrid vehicle has two sources of power – an internal combustion engine (ICE) and an electric motor. The wheels can be driven by the engine, the motor or both at the same time. An ICE has high torque at high speeds but low torque at low speeds and therefore wastes a lot of energy when the vehicle is stationary or moves off. An electric motor has maximum torque the moment it starts to turn so it is ideally suited to power a vehicle from rest. In a hybrid vehicle, a computer with an energy monitoring function calculates the best energy source at any time and switches the engine and the motor on and off, as necessary. At the traffic lights, for example, when the vehicle is stationary, the ICE and the electric motor are switched off, so no power is wasted. However, as soon as the driver accelerates from a lower to a higher speed, the ICE kicks in and the vehicle is driven by both power sources. At low speeds (e.g. up to 70–80 km/h) when the vehicle isn't accelerating, only the electric motor is needed to turn the wheels. When the vehicle slows down or the driver puts the brakes on, very little power is lost because the energy which is not needed to turn the wheels is used to power a generator which recharges the battery. This is called regenerative braking.

acceleration • low speed • regenerative braking • stationary

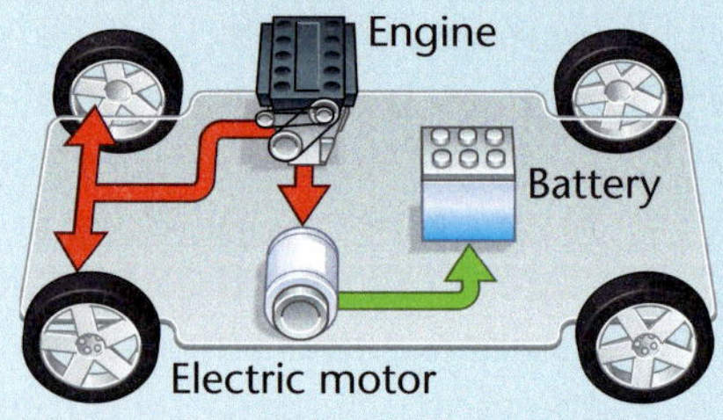

A ______________________

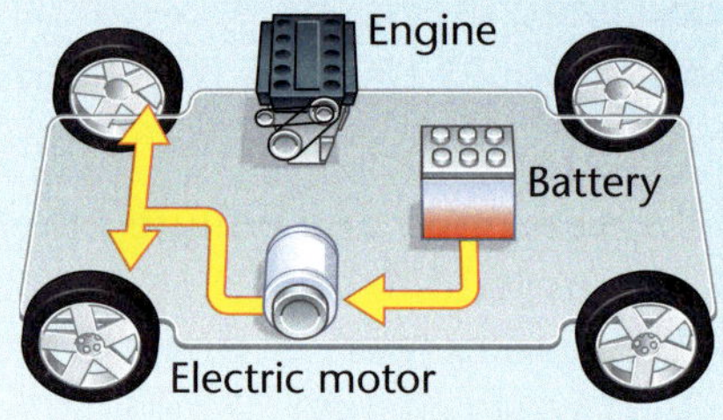

B ______________________

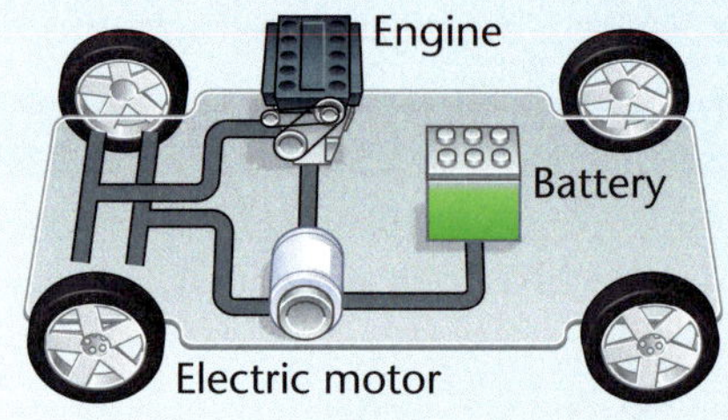

C ______________________

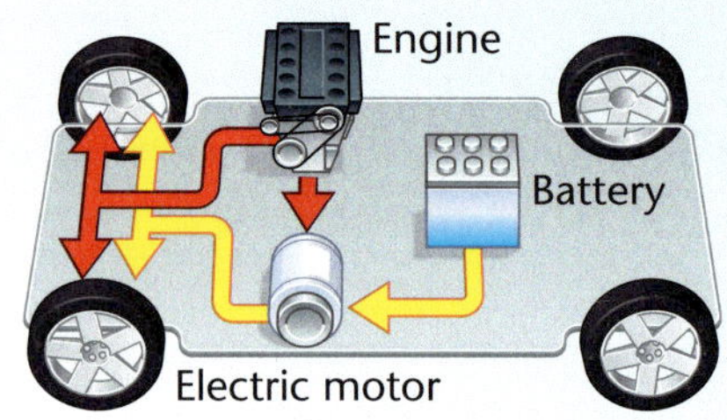

D ______________________

2 Choose the right word to complete the sentences.

1 The wheels of a hybrid vehicle are
- **a** always driven by one power source.
- **b** always driven by two power sources.
- **c** sometimes driven by two power sources.

2 An ICE is more efficient at
- **a** low speeds.
- **b** high speeds.
- **c** all speeds.

3 An electric motor
- **a** has full power at low speeds.
- **b** only has full power at low speeds.
- **c** only has full power at high speeds.

4 The computer switches on a hybrid's petrol engine
- **a** when the car speeds up quickly.
- **b** when the car is stationary.
- **c** at low speeds.

3 Use words from the text to fill in the gaps.

The oldest ________________ [1] vehicle on the market is the Toyota Prius. It has both an electric motor and a petrol ________________ [2]. The motor has high ________________ [3] at low speeds, so when the car ________________ [4] off, the electric motor is the ________________ [5] of power. This system is very efficient and little power is ________________ [6]. However, as soon as the car ________________ [7], the petrol engine ________________ [8] in but when the vehicle slows down again the ________________ [9] braking system ________________ [10] the battery.

4 The taxi drivers' comments on this Internet discussion forum are mixed up. There are three statements and 3 reactions to these statements. Re-arrange the comments in logical pairs.

This month we're sharing our thoughts about hybrid taxis. Tell us what's on your mind!

A	Those hi-tech nickel-metal hydride batteries in hybrids cost between $5,000–$10,000! Are you prepared to spend all that money on just one car component? And isn't nickel a heavy metal? *Nancy, San Antonio, Texas, USA*
B	The temperature is sometimes well below zero here but I still drove 300,000 miles on my hybrid's original battery. I'm not planning to change to a regular cab. No way! *Andrew, Vancouver, BC, Canada*
C	I agree that electricity is a clean and quiet source of energy but think of how it's generated! What fuel does your power station use? If it's coal-fired, we're back to where we started. *Fiona, Edinburgh, UK*
D	Why has no one mentioned the environment? Hybrids are so quiet you can't hear them at all when they're stationary. Their fuel consumption is only about 4 litres per 100 kilometres and they emit as little as 93 g/km of CO_2. These facts speak for themselves. *Tom, London, UK*
E	You get your money back in no time at all! Here in San Francisco we have calculated that averaging 90,000 miles per year, each cab saves $9,000 on gasoline*. *Don, San Francisco, California, USA*
F	Why is everyone talking about electric motors? Anyone who did physics at school knows that a battery loses its power when it gets cold. Have you thought about that? *Rashid, Accra, India*

A + ________, ________ + ________, ________ + ________

* AE: gasoline, BE: petrol

5 For and against: With a partner make a list in an exercise book of the advantages and disadvantages of hybrid vehicles. Add your own ideas then say why you would or wouldn't buy a hybrid. Present your findings to the class.

Electromagnetic control of currents

1 Label the diagram of a contactor with the highlighted words from the text.

A contactor is an electromagnetic switch. It uses a low current to switch on a more powerful current, e.g. to operate a 3-phase induction motor. In a contactor, a **control circuit** energizes the contactor's **coils** which produce a magnetic field in the **core**. The magnetic field makes the **armature** move towards the contactor's core and when the armature moves, its two **movable contacts** touch the **stationary contacts** of the **power circuit**, which is then completed. A contactor has normally open (N/O) contacts because they are held apart by **springs** as long as there is no magnetic field.

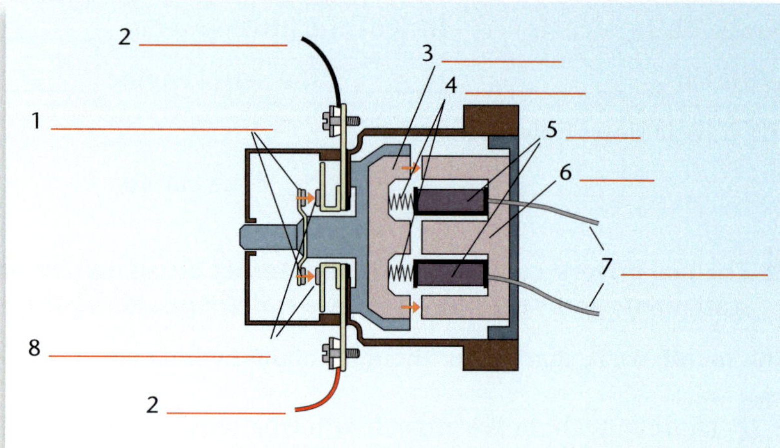

T15 2 Make a table with 3 columns in an exercise book. The titles of the columns are: Position, Function and Number. Now listen to the electrician explaining how to install a car relay for the fog lights.

3 Use the switchboard below to explain what will happen when voltage is applied to relays 1–3.

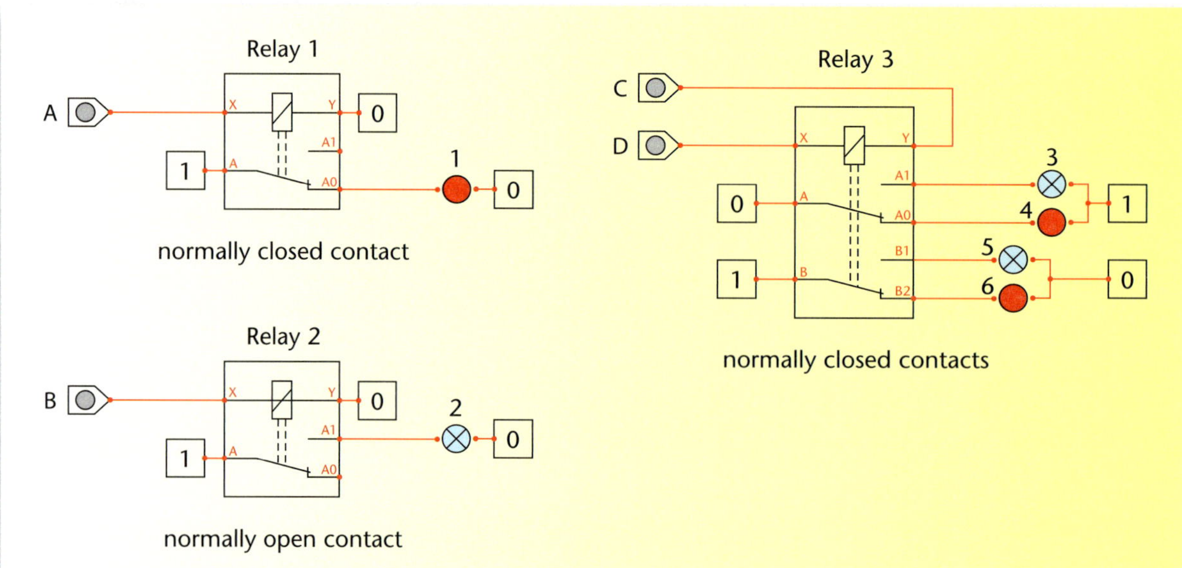

When relay 1 2 3	is activated by	switch A/B/…, both switches,	light bulb 1/2 light bulbs … and …	is are	switched	on. off.

T16 **4 Troubleshooting: The conveyor belt in a warehouse keeps on stopping. Listen to the dialogue and fill in the gaps.**

1 The conveyor belt keeps on ______________________________.
2 They conveyor belt has a separate switching unit with a ______________________.
3 Martin and Lari have got a ______________________________ diagram.
4 It's a ______________________________ induction motor.
5 Lari thinks that one of the fuses has ______________________________.
6 With a contactor you can use a ____________ current to control a circuit with a high current.
7 The word they can see on the contactor is "____________________".
8 The contactor has a motor ______________________ function.
9 The overload heater contacts are normally ____________________.
10 The motor is overheating because it hasn't been ____________________ for years.

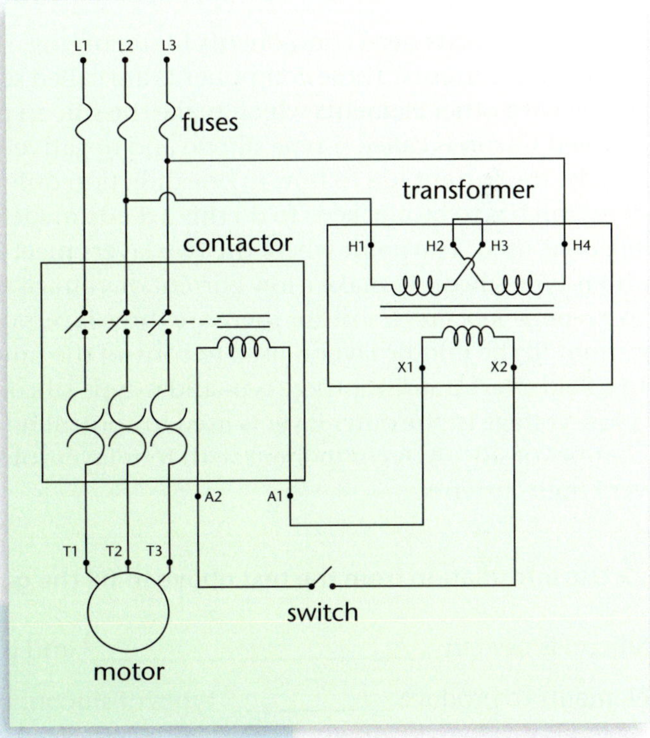

5 Use the expressions in the box to write a description of the schematic diagram in exercise 4.

- It consists of ...
- It is made up of ...
- Current enters the ...
- The curent passes through the ...
- The contactor gets its current from ...
- The current in the ... is higher/lower than the current in ...
- The contacts in the ... are normally open/closed.
- When the switch is thrown, the coil ...
- When the switching circuit is completed, ...
- If the overload heaters trip, they ...
-
- attract ≠ repel switch on ≠ switch off

6 With a partner prepare a short presentation of another circuit (e.g. from your German electrical engineering textbook).

Electronic control of currents

1 Use the highlighted words in the text to label the diagrams.

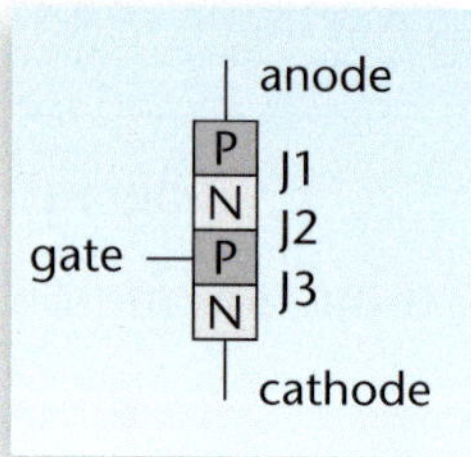

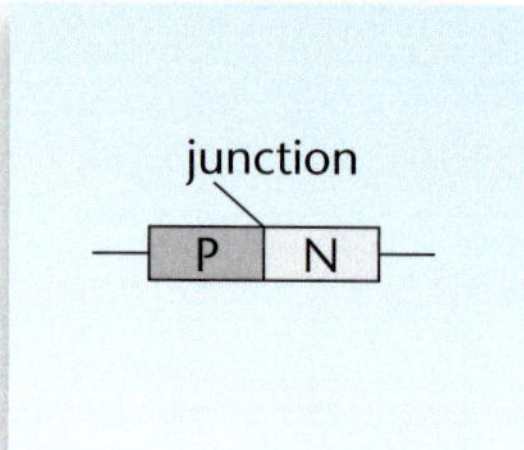

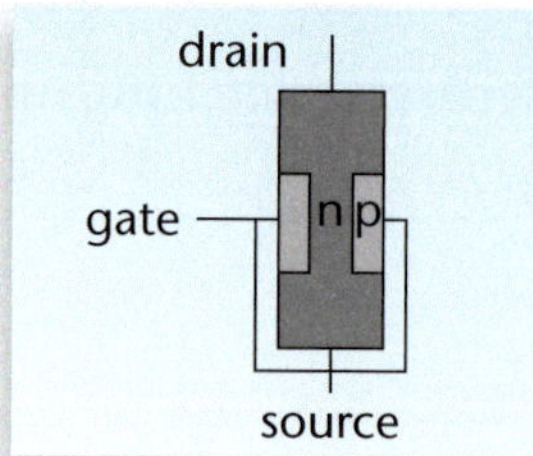

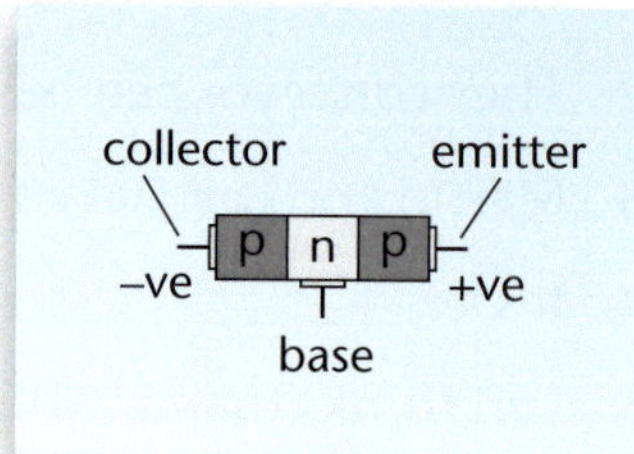

1 ____________ 2 ____________ 3 ____________ 4 ____________

Electronic circuits need components for rectifying, switching, blocking, diverting and amplifying currents. These components are called semiconductors and are often made of silicon mixed with other elements which make the silicon positively or negatively charged. Positively charged silicon is called p-type silicon and negatively charged is called n-type. In some electrical circuits the current has to flow in one direction only and the current flowing in the opposite direction has to be blocked. To do this a **diode** made of one layer of p-type and one of n-type silicon is used. The point where the two layers meet is called the junction. A transistors uses p- and n-type silicon to make a low current or voltage amplify, switch or control a stronger current. In a **bipolar junction transistor** there are three layers of silicon separated by two junctions. A small current in the middle layer is used to control the much stronger current in the other two layers. In a **field effect transistor** there is p- and n-type silicon but one type is wrapped around the other. A low voltage in the outer layer is used to control how much current passes through the central channel of silicon. A component with four layers of silicon called a **thyristor** is used to switch very high currents.

2 Use information from the text above to fill the gaps.

Silicon is used in ____________ 1 and is ____________ 2 with other elements to produce ____________ 3 types of silicon. In a diode two ____________ 4 of silicon meet at a junction. A bipolar transistor has ____________ 5 junctions. In a ____________ 6 effect transistor there is a central ____________ 7 through which the current passes. Very high currents are switched by a ____________ 8, which has ____________ 9 layers of silicon.

3 Use your electrical engineering textbook to match the symbols with the names.

thyristor • field effect transistor • bipolar junction transistor • diode

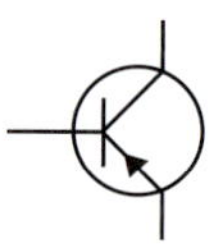

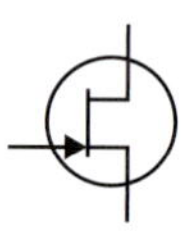

1 ____________ 2 ____________ 3 ____________ 4 ____________

4 Can you understand a schematic? Work in pairs to locate and name the components in the box. Begin like this:

Where's the capacitor? It's in square … (e.g. A5).

bridge rectifier ______________
capacitor ______________
diode(s) ______________
fuse(s) ______________
resistor(s) ______________
transformer ______________
transistor ______________
Zener diode ______________

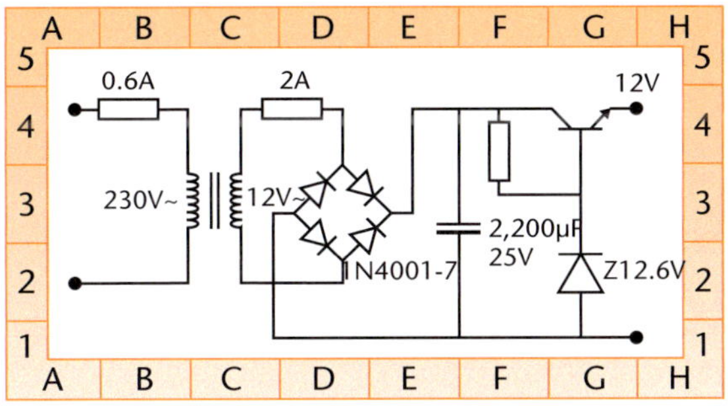

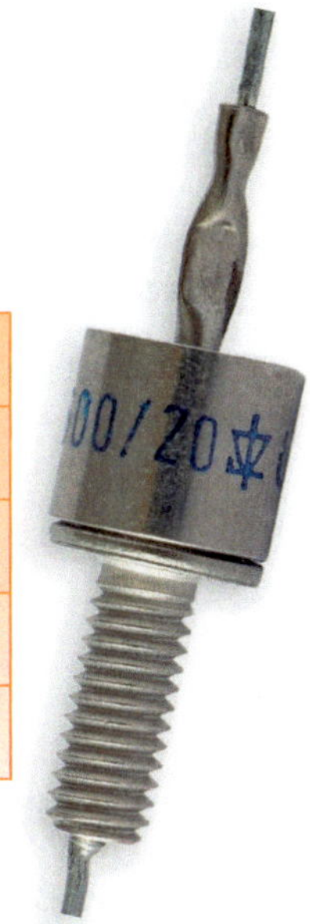

5 Write a sentence explaining what each component in the above circuit does.

A	capacitor diode fuse transformer resistor transistor	amplifies blocks limits protects rectifies smooths steps stops stores switches	a component. a current. a current up and down. an electric charge. an overcurrent. a signal.

1 ______________________________
2 ______________________________
3 ______________________________
4 ______________________________
5 ______________________________
6 ______________________________

T17

6 What is the circuit above for? To find out listen to the dialogue in which an apprentice electrician asks a colleague for help with a circuit. Fill in the table as you listen.

Correct component	Type	Maximum rating
Diode		
Transistor		
Function of the circuit		

Control systems

1 Open and closed loop control systems. Read the text and match the sentence halves.

Central heating system

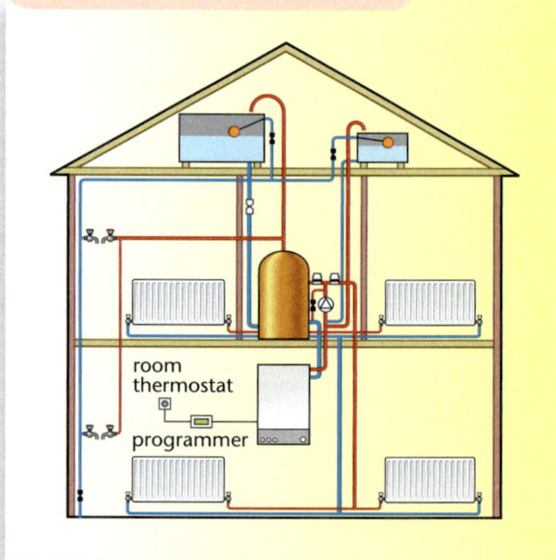

The simplest control system is a toggle switch, which is either on or off. In a simple lighting circuit the switch completes the circuit and turns the light bulb on. There is no feedback to the switch to break the circuit if, for example, the light is too bright or the bulb blows. This is an example of an open loop control system.
However, a typical central heating system works on a different principle. The householder selects a temperature, the system switches the heater on until the desired temperature is reached and then there is feedback to the system which switches the heater off again. When the temperature becomes too low, there is more feedback to the switch to turn the heater back on again. This type of system is called a closed loop control system.
A closed loop control system can have a discontinuous or a continuous action controller. In the case of an electric iron, for example, a bimetallic strip makes or breaks the circuit depending on the temperature of the iron. This type of control system is inexact and slow and is an example of a two-position, discontinuous action controller. If, however, the temperature of a liquid in a steam-heated tank is to be kept absolutely constant, a different system is needed. In such cases a sensor continuously registers the temperature of the liquid and sends signals back to the motor operating the valve to let more, less or no steam in. In this way the temperature stays constant. This is an example of a continuous action controller.

1 An on/off switch is an example of
2 An open loop control system isn't
3 An open loop control system
4 A closed loop control system
5 A discontinuous action controller reacts
6 A continuous action controller uses
7 Continuous action control is more
8 The temperature in a two-position closed loop temperature control system

A is always between a maximum and minimum value.
B slowly.
C exact than a discontinuous action control.
D constant feedback.
E an open loop controller.
F always uses feedback.
G normally used in a typical central system.
H never uses feedback.

1___ 2___ 3___ 4___ 5___ 6___ 7___ 8___

2 Read the text and then label the parts of the mercury switch with the highlighted words.

The mercury switch in the diagram switches a **heater** on and an **air conditioner** off. It is made of a **glass vial** which has a **common contact** at the bottom running from left to right. At the moment this contact is connected by a small quantity of **mercury** to the wire leading to the air conditioner. The vial is attached to a **thermometer coil** with a **lever** in the middle. The coil is a bimetallic strip. If the temperature now goes down, the bimetallic strip will contract, the glass vial will tip to the left and the mercury will run to the left, switch off the air conditioner and switch on the heater.

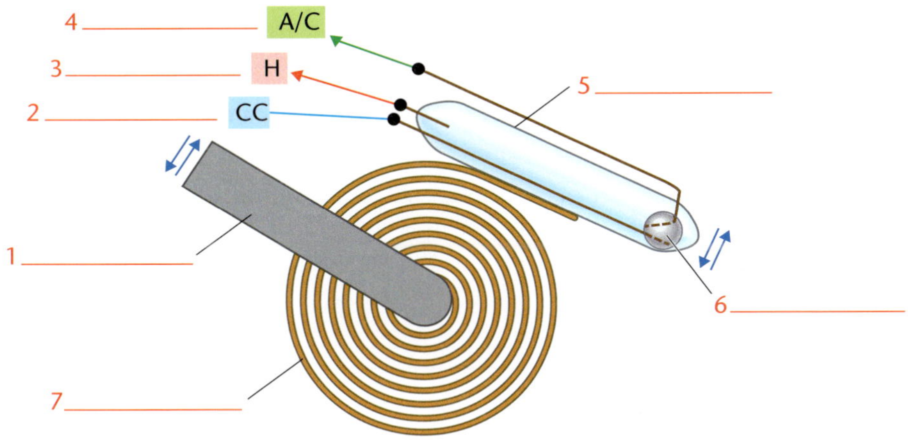

3 **Open or closed loop?**
In an exercise book, put these devices in the right columns.

bimetallic strip • contactor • cruise control • digital thermostat • dimmer • mercury switch • relay • washing machine program switch

T18 4 **Listen to the description of how a cruise control system works and complete the table.**

1 ______________________
2 ______________________
3 ______________________
4 ______________________
5 ______________________
6 ______________________
7 ______________________
8 ______________________
9 ______________________

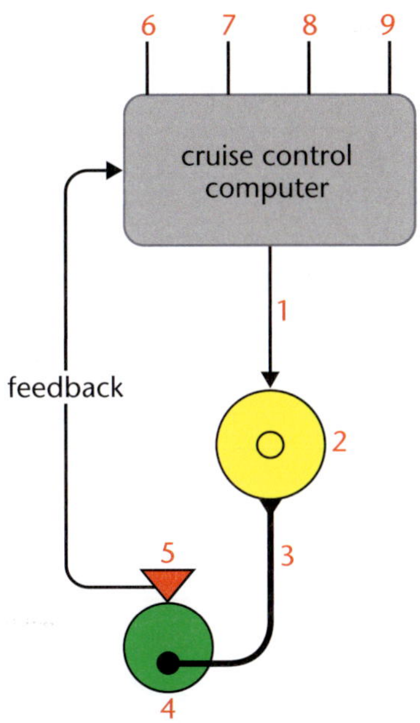

5 **Presentation. With a partner give a presentation of a car's speed control system.**
Look at the handbook or on the Internet and use the expressions below.

If you press the … (e.g. accelerate / off / set) button, the vehicle … (e.g. will go faster / slow down / stay at the current speed). The … (e.g. "resume") button makes the vehicle … (e.g. go back to the last speed setting). You can accelerate / slow down by + -ing (e.g. tapping the plus / minus button).

Sensors

1 Read the text and write the names of the highlighted parts in the diagram.

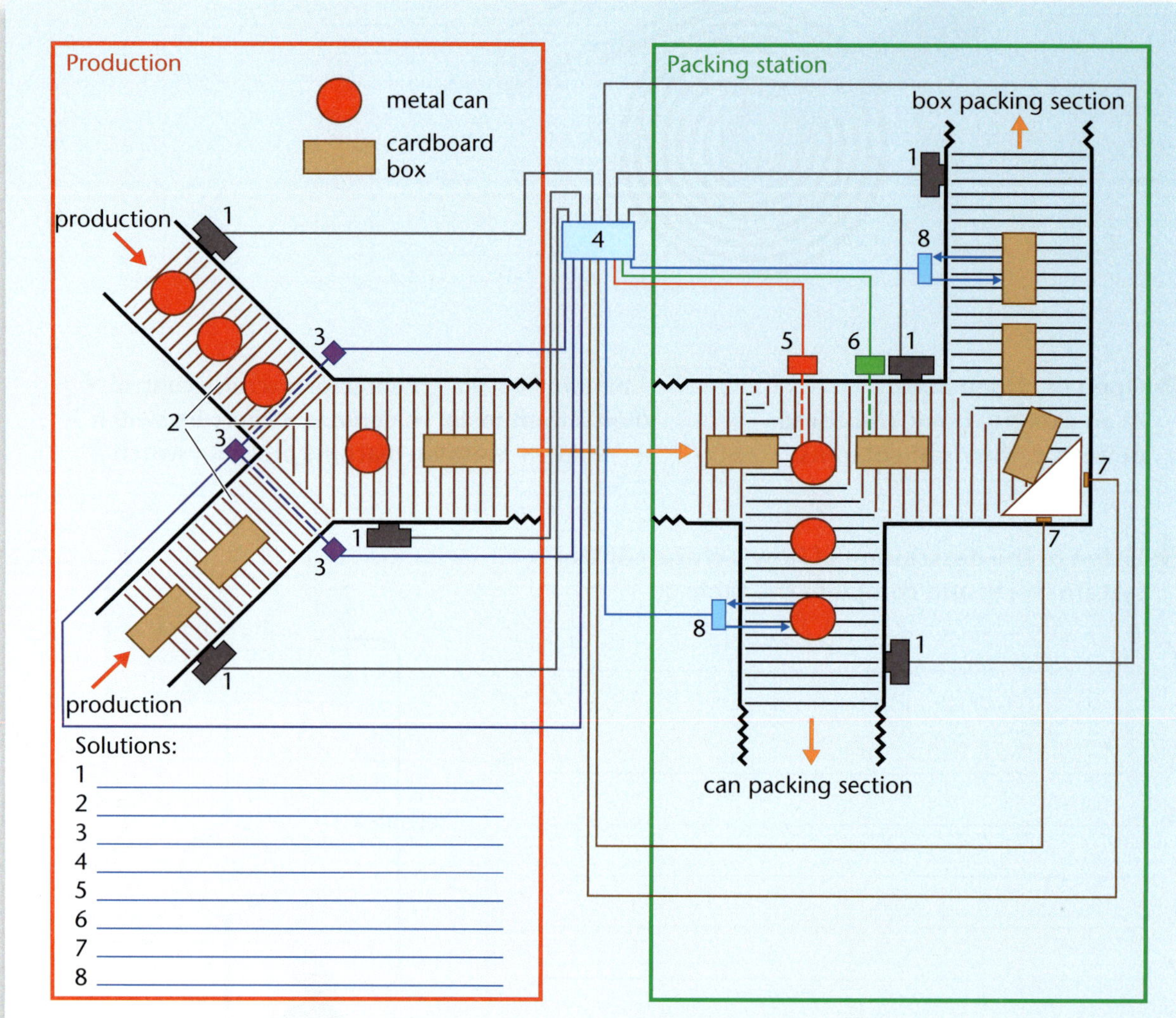

Solutions:
1 ____
2 ____
3 ____
4 ____
5 ____
6 ____
7 ____
8 ____

Modern manufacturing processes use programmable logic controllers (PLCs) to regulate material flow. In the diagrams above, the **PLC** controls the speed at which metal cans and cardboard boxes from the production hall of a factory are transported on **conveyor belts** to the packing station. The PLC's job is to control the six **electric motors** which drive the belts and it does this by using data from different types of sensors. When the cans and boxes leave production they first pass through two **photoelectric proximity sensors** which stop and start the belts to make sure there is enough room for the objects on the next belt. When the metal cans and cardboard boxes reach the packing station, an **inductive proximity sensor** recognises the metal in the cans and activates a belt to transport them to the can packing section. Next a **capacitive proximity sensor** detects the non-conductive cardboard and switches on the belt to the box packing section. If too many cardboard boxes build up, they press against the triangular corner piece. This activates one or both of the two **limit switches** which react to direct pressure and switch off the belt so the blockage can be cleared. Finally, an **ultrasonic sensor** is used to count the cans and boxes.

2 Complete the definitions with words from the text.

1 In a modern factory conveyor belts are controlled by ______________________.
2 A ______________________ proximity sensor reacts to light.
3 An ______________________ proximity sensor only reacts to metals.
4 A ______________________ proximity sensor can recognise cardboard.
5 A ______________________ switch reacts if it is touched.
6 An ______________________ sensor uses sound waves.

T19

3 Listen to the guided tour of a food-processing factory and then say if the following statements are true or false. Correct the false statements in an exercise book.

1 Mike begins by showing them a video.
2 The canning machine is operated by robots.
3 The sensor for the soup-canning machinery uses sound waves.
4 The conveyor belt has the same type of sensor as the canning machinery.
5 The sensor for the roll of plastic film is like the one for the conveyor belt.
6 They finish the tour by having a meal in the canteen.

4 A guided tour: in your exercise book write these expressions from the recording under the 4 headings above. There are three for each heading.

Greeting the visitors	Structuring the tour	Explaining	Finishing the tour
…	…	…	…

Here you can see how … • I very much hope you enjoyed it. • If you'd like any more information, I'll be pleased to help. • I'll be your guide this morning. • I'm going to start with … • My name's … • Our next stop is … • The … (e.g. sensor) consists of … • The next thing I want to show you is … • Well, we've come to the end of our tour … • … (e.g. "PLC") stands for … • Good morning and welcome to …

5 Role play: Prepare a guided tour of your workplace for a group of English-speaking visitors. Then act it out in front of the other members of your class.

GUIDE/GUIDES

Good … and welcome to …
My name is/Our names are …
Before we start, we'd like to give each of you a name tag/brochure/…
The toilets/restrooms are …
We're going to start with a video/…
We'll start the tour at/in the …
We'll walk from here to the …
Please follow me.
Please be careful.
Please don't touch the …
Would anyone like a coffee/poster/…?
Are there any questions?

VISITORS

Excuse me, is there a toilet/restroom …?
Could you explain what a … is, please?
What does this thing/device/… do?
I'd/We'd like to know more about the …?
How does this work?
How many people work here?
Who is responsible for …?
Do you have a quality control department/…?
is it always this noisy/quiet/clean/dirty/…?
How many … do you produce in a day/…?
We're especially interested in …
I'm sorry, I didn't catch that.
Can you repeat that, please?

Job applications

1 Read the job advert and choose the correct statements.

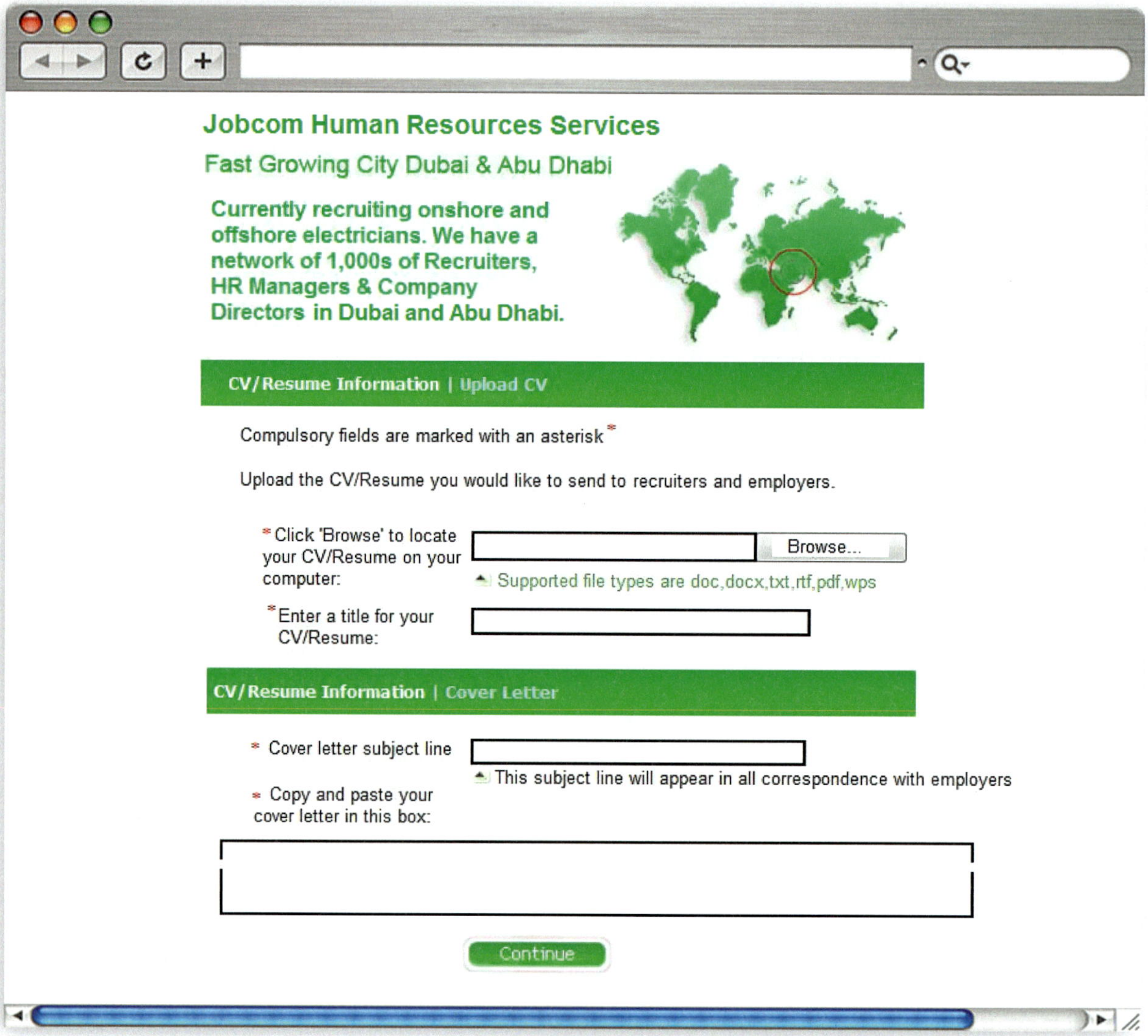

1 Dubai and Abu Dhabi are
- **a** in Africa.
- **b** in the Middle East.
- **c** in South America.

2 This is an advert by
- **a** an oil company.
- **b** the cities of Dubai and Abu Dhabi.
- **c** a recruitment agency.

3 An HR manager works with
- **a** people.
- **b** electricity.
- **c** oil.

4 On this web page you have to fill in
- **a** 2 boxes.
- **b** 3 boxes.
- **c** 4 boxes.

5 To get a job with this company you need
- **a** 1 document.
- **b** 2 documents.
- **c** 3 documents.

6 A CV or resume has details of
- **a** the jobs you want.
- **b** the training you want.
- **c** your education, training and skills.

2 **How is this CV/resume different from a German 'Lebenslauf'? Discuss it with a group and make a list of the differences.**

There's no reference to ...

There isn't a ...

Why isn't there a photo?

Curriculum Vitae

Personal Details

Name:	Frank Hinz
Date of birth:	10 February[1] 1989
Gender:	Male
Nationality:	German
Marital status	Single
Address:	Bahnhofst, 12, 44892 Bochum, Germany
Land line:	[2] +49 234 7659231
Mobile phone:	+49 177 63384520
E-mail:	frank.hinz@gmail.com

Profile

Newly qualified electrician seeking post abroad. [3]
Good spoken and written English. Mobile and flexible. [4]

Education and Training

2006 - 2009	3-year traineeship at Siemens AG, Essen and Dr Georg Schäfer [5] Vocational Training College in Bochum, Germany.
June 2006	German Class 10 School Leaving Certificate
1994 – 2004	[6] Primary and secondary education in Bochum

Work Experience

Since 2006	Experience of installing, maintaining and repairing electrical systems (household and industrial wiring) and motors
2005	5-day placement at Elektro Fischer (local electrical contractor) doing maintenance and repairs of industrial wiring

Relevant Skills [7]

Full driving licence
First aid certificate
Life saving certificate

Extra-curricular Activities [8]

Voluntary member of local fire and rescue service
Captain of local soccer team
Active member of church community service group
Deep-sea diving

Erläuterungen

1. Monat immer ausschreiben.
2. Das Pluszeichen ersetzt den Auslandscode 00.
3. Hier erfährt der Arbeitgeber auf einen Blick, wer der Bewerber ist und was er will.
4. Die Beherrschung einer Fremdsprache wird mit *fluent*, *good* und *basic* beschrieben.
5. Alle deutschen Begriffe (z. B. Berufsschule) sind ins Englische zu übersetzen.
6. Eine knappe Bezeichnung der schulischen Laufbahn reicht für eine handwerkliche Tätigkeit.
7. Alle weiteren für das Arbeiten im Ausland relevanten Fähigkeiten sind hier zu erwähnen.
8. Alle außerschulischen Aktivitäten, die Aufschluss über die Persönlichkeit des Bewerbers geben, sind anzugeben.

3 Now write your own CV in the same format as the example above.

4 Choose the right headings from the CV for the following information. There are two examples for each heading.

Information	Heading
A highly motivated and hard-working	______
B sound engineer for rock band	______
C week's placement with local electrical contractor	______
D motorcycle licence	______
E divorced	______
F 2½-year apprenticeship at Thyssen AG in Essen	______
G I wish to gain experience of working outdoors.	______
H pizza-taxi driver	______
I heavy goods vehicle driving licence	______
J German higher education entrance qualifications	______
K member of the Red Cross	______
L married	______

5 Explaining German expressions. Match the German on the left with the English on the right.

1 Allgemeine Hochschulreife (Abitur)
2 Ausbildung, Lehre
3 Azubi, Lehrling
4 Berufsschule, Berufskolleg, Gewerbliche Schule
5 Elektroniker
6 Energieelektroniker
7 Fachhochschulreife
8 Führerschein Klasse 3
9 Mittlere Reife
10 Sekundarstufe 1 und 2
11 Wehrdienst
12 Zivildienst

A car licence
B German university entrance qualifications
C German higher education entrance qualifications
D secondary education
E German Class 10 School Leaving Certificate
F electronics technician
G trainee, apprentice
H (BE) vocational training college, (AE) vocational school
I community service
J military service
K energy electronics technician
L traineeship, apprenticeship

1___ **2**___ **3**___ **4**___ **5**___ **6**___ **7**___ **8**___ **9**___ **10**___ **11**___ **12**___

6 Maik Althoff applies for the job in this advert. Use words from the list to fill in the gaps in his cover letter on the next page.

Are you looking for adventure?
If you are, come and work in the offshore drilling industry for Outriggers International!
You – are a qualified electrician, 20–45 years old, speak good English and aren't afraid of hard work in a tough environment
We – pay top rates, train you on the job, work in the Persian Gulf, the Gulf of Mexico and the North Sea.
Upload your CV/resume in the box below and e-mail your cover letter to bill.ridges@outrigger.com. If you're the person we're looking for, we'll be in touch.

apprenticeship • available • cables • experience • interested • licensed • motivated • notice • offshore • position

Dear Mr Ridges

I am very ______________[1] in working as an electrician in the ______________[2] drilling industry. By July 20… I will have completed my 3-year ______________[3] at Heller Starkstromtechnik GmbH in Freiburg and will then be a ______________[4] electrician. I have ______________[5] of installing and maintaining overhead power ______________[6] for trams in Germany, Denmark, France and the Netherlands.

My English is good and I am highly ______________[7] and flexible.

I am ______________[8] for interview at short ______________[9] in person or on the telephone and very much hope you will consider me for this ______________[10].

Yours sincerely

Maik Althoff

7 Maik Althoff applies for the job with Outriggers International and one evening a few days later he gets a telephone call. What does the caller say?

Maik Althoff: Ja, hallo?
Caller: Good evening. My name is Bill Ridges of Outriggers International. Am I …? [1]
Maik Althoff: Yes, my name is Maik Althoff. Can you say your name again, please?
Caller: … [2]
Maik Althoff: Oh yes, now I remember. You're from Outriggers International.
Caller: Yes, that's right. Have you got a few minutes to …? [3]
Maik Althoff: Yes, I'll try to answer any questions you have. I hope my English will be good enough!
Caller: I'm sure it will be, Mr Althoff. Could you …? [4]
Maik Althoff: It's not very easy to describe my work on trams because I don't know all the words in English.
Caller: Can …, for example? [5]
Maik Althoff: Yes, I can tell you something about safety. Safety is very important. We always wear orange overalls and steel ladders are not allowed.
Caller: Thank you. I have one more question. Are you prepared …? [6]
Maik Althoff: 6 months at a time on an oil rig is a long time, but I'm prepared to do that. Yes, I would be prepared to live away from home for 6 months.
Caller: Good. Thanks for answering my questions, Mr Althoff. Have …? [7]
Maik Althoff: Well, er, I can't think of any at the moment. Perhaps later.
Caller: Very well. Will … sometime next week, Mr Althoff? [8]
Maik Althoff: Yes, certainly.
Caller: Fine. I'll send … details. [9] Goodbye for now.
Maik Althoff: Goodbye.

T 20 **Now listen to the recording and check your answers.**

Die Zahlen geben die Quelle des Wortes an, z. B. anode *2.1* = Unit 2, Aufgabe 1

A
accelerate *14.2 – beschleunigen*
accumulator *2.1 – Akku(mulator)*
acid paste *2.1 – Säurepaste*
adventure *20.6 – Abenteuer*
advert *20.1 – Inserat, Anzeige*
air shaft *13.3 – Luftschacht*
alarm *5.5 – Alarmanlage; alarmieren*
alternating current *3.1 – Wechselstrom*
amplify *17.5 – verstärken*
amplifying *17.1 – Verstärken*
angle grinder *4.5 – Winkelschleifer*
anode *2.1 – Anode, positiver Pol*
antenna *5.1 – Antenne*
appliance *2.5 – Gerät, Anwendung*
application *3.7 – Ver-, Anwendung*
application (for a job) *20.1 – Bewerbung (um eine Stelle)*
apply for a job *20.7 – sich um eine Stelle bewerben*
apprentice *17.6 – auszubildende/r*
armature *3.1 – Armatur, Anker*
assume *8.5 – annehmen, davon ausgehen*
atomic particle *1.1 – Atomteilchen*
attract *1.1 – (sich) anziehen*
available *11.1 – erhältlich, verfügbar*
average *1.2 – Durchschnitt; durchschnittlich*
axle *12.2 – Achse*

B
bare wire *10.2 – blanker Draht*
battery *1.1 – Batterie*
battery pack *14.2 – Akku(mulator)*
be attached to *5.4 – verbunden sein mit*
be called *2.1 – heißen*
be connected to/by *2.1 – verbunden sein mit/durch*
be dead (battery) 2.1 *– leer sein*
be defined as *4.1 – definiert sein als*
be in touch *20.6 – sich melden*
be measured in *1.2 – gemessen werden in*
be reversed by *2.1 – rückgängig gemacht werden durch*
be suited to *15.1 – geeignet sein für*
belt sander *4.5 – Schwingschleifer*
bend open *12.1 – aufbiegen*
bipolar junction transistor *17.1 – zweipoliger Schichttransistor*
blackout *7.3 – Stromausfall*
blade fuse *9.1 – Sicherung mit Messerkontakten*
block of wood *12.1 – Holzblock, -klotz*
block sth *10.2 – etw blockieren, absperren*
blocking *17.1 – Blockieren, Sperren*
blow a fuse *9.1 – durchbrennen*
bolt of lightning *1.2 – Blitzstrahl*
boost *8.2 – erhöhen, verstärken*
bridge rectifier *17.4 – Brückengleichrichter*
brush (contact) *4.5 – (Kontakt-)Bürste, Stromabnehmer*
buried cable *10.2 – unterirdisches Kabel*
button cell *2.5 – Knopfzelle*

C
cab *15.4 – Taxi*
calculate *15.1 – berechnen*
calculator *7.3 – Taschenrechner*
camera flash unit *8.1 – Blitzgerät*
can *19.1 – Dose, Büchse*
canning machinery *19.3 – Füllanlage*
capacitive proximity sensor *19.1 – kapazitiver Näherungssensor*
capacitor *5.1 – Kondensator*
car aerial *13.4 – Autoantenne*
car dashboard *11.3 – Armaturenbrett*
car relay *16.2 – Autorelais*
car seat-positioning motor *13.4 – Motor zur Sitzverstellung*
carbon *2.1 – Kohlenstoff*
cardboard *19.1 – Pappe*
cartridge fuse *9.1 – Patronensicherung*
casing *2.1 – Gehäuse*
I didn't catch that. 19.5 *– Ich habe das nicht mitbekommen.*
catch fire *9.1 – Feuer fangen, in Brand geraten*
cathode *2.1 – Kathode, negativer Pol*
ceiling *11.2 – Decke, Decken-*
CFL *11.3 – Energiesparlampe*
chain reaction *7.2 – Kettenreaktion*
change gear *14.2 – in einen anderen Gang schalten*
channel *17.1 – Kanal*
charge *2.1 – (auf)laden (von Akkumulatoren, Kondensatoren)*
charged particles *1.2 – geladene Teilchen*
chart *11.5 – Diagramm, Tabelle*
chemical reaction *8.1 – chemische Reaktion*
circuit *1.2 – Schaltung, Kreislauf, (Strom-) Kreis*
circuit-breaker *7.4 – Leitungsschutzschalter*
circular movement *3.1 – Kreisbewegung*
closed loop control *18.1 – geschlossener Regelkreis*
coal-fired *15.4 – mit Kohlefeuerung*
coil *3.5 – Windung, Spule, Spirale*
colleague *10.4 – Kollege/Kollegin*
colour rendition *11.1 – Farbwiedergabe*
commercial *2.1 – handelsüblich*
common contact *18.2 – gemeinsamer Kontakt*
community service *20.2 – gemeinnützige Tätigkeit, Zivildienst*
commutator *4.5 – Kollektor, Stromwender*
component *5.1 – Bauteil*
compressed air *8.1 – Druckluft*
compressor *13.4 – Kompressor*
conductor *1.1 – Leiter*
connect *4.1 – (miteinander) verbinden, anschließen*
consist of *5.4 – bestehen aus*
consumer *6.1 – Verbraucher/in, Konsument/in*
contactor *16.1 – Kontakt-, Impulsgeber*
continuous action controller *18.1 – kontinuierliche Regeleinrichtung*
contract *18.2 – (sich) zusammenziehen*
contractor *20.2 – Unternehmer (mit Werkvertrag)*
control circuit *16.1 – Steuerkreis*
conveyor belt *16.4 – Fließ-, Förderband*
cooker *7.3 – (Elektro-)Herd*
copper *1.1 – Kupfer; kupfern*
copper wire *1.1 – Kupferdraht*
cordless drill *4.3 – Akku-Schrauber, -Bohrer*
core *16.1 – Kern*
correspondence *20.1 – Briefwechsel, Korrespondenz*
cosmetic use *11.1 – kosmetische Verwendung*
cover letter *20.1 – Begleitschreiben, -brief*
crossword (puzzle) *13.2 – Kreuzworträtsel*
cruise control *18.3 – Tempomat*
crystal earpiece *5.1 – Kristallhörer*
current *1.1 – Strom, Strömung*
curriculum vitæ/resume *20.1 – Lebenslauf*
customer *6.6 – Kunde/Kundin*

D
decoration *11.1 – Dekoration*
deep-sea diving *20.2 – Tiefseetauchen*
demonstrate *3.5 – demonstrieren, zeigen*
destination *7.1 – Ziel, Bestimmungsort*
device *4.3 – Vorrichtung, Gerät, Apparat*
dimmable *11.1 – dimmbar*
diode *5.1 – Diode*
direct current *2.1 – Gleichstrom*
direction *3.1 – Richtung*
disconnect *7.4 – trennen, herausziehen*
discontinuous action controller *18.1 – unterbrochene Regeleinrichtung*
dishwasher *8.5 – Geschirrspüler*
diverting *17.1 – Ablenken*
divided by *6.1 – geteilt durch*
divorced *20.4 – geschieden*
drill *12.1 – Bohrer, Bohrmaschine; bohren*
drilling industry *20.6 – Ölbohrindustrie*
dry cell battery *2.1 – Trockenbatterie*
dynamo *3.1 – Lichtmaschine, Dynamo*

E
earth-moving machinery *10.2 – Erdbaumaschinen, Großgerät*
efficiency *11.1 Wirkungsgrad*
efficient *8.2 – effizient, wirksam*
electric charge *1.1 – elektrische Ladung*
electric cooker *8.5 – Elektroherd*
electric fan *13.4 – elektrischer Ventilator*
electric generator *3.1 – Stromgenerator*
electric heater 9.3 *– Elektroheizung, elektrisches Heizgerät*
electric iron *18.1 – elektrisches Bügeleisen*
electric jigsaw *4.5 – elektrische Stichsäge*
electrical contractor *6.6 – Elektroinstallateur*
electrical engineer *9.1 – Elektroingenieur/in*
electricity *1.1 – Elektrizität, Strom*
electrocardiograph *7.3 – Elektrokardiograph*
electromagnetic *16.1 – elektromagnetisch*
electron *1.1 – Elektron*
electronic *4.5 – elektronisch*
element *17.1 – Element*
emission *14.2 – Emission, Ausstoß, Abgase*
emit *15.4 – emittieren, ausstoßen*
employer *20.1 – Arbeitgeber/in*
encoder *14.1 – Kodiergerät, Impulsgeber*
energize *16.1 – aufladen*
energy *1.2 – Energie*
energy-efficient *11.1 – energiesparend*
energy monitoring *15.1 – Energiekontrolle*
equation *6.4 – Gleichung*
equipment *9.1 – Geräte, Maschinen*
experience *20.2 – (Berufs-)Erfahrung*
experiment *3.5 – Versuch, Experiment; experimentieren*
explanation *3.3 – Erklärung*
explode *11.1 – explodieren*
expression *6.5 – Ausdruck*
external *2.1 – Außen-, von außen*
extra curricular activity *20.2 – außerschulische Aktivität*
extractor fan 9.3 *– Entlüfter, Abzugshaube*

F

factor 11.5 – *Faktor*
fail 7.2 – *versagen , ausfallen*
faulty 9.1 – *fehlerhaft, defekt*
feedback 18.1 – *Rückmeldung*
field-effect transistor 17.1 – *Feldeffekt-Transistor*
filament 4.1 – *(Glüh-)Faden*
film projector 11.1 – *Filmprojektor*
fire and rescue service 20.2 – *Feuerwehr und Rettungsdienst*
flexible 20.2 – *flexibel*
floodlight 11.1 – *Flutlicht*
flow 1.1 – *fließen*
fluorescent tube 11.4 – *Leuchtröhre*
fog light 16.2 – *Nebelscheinwerfer*
force 1.1 – *Kraft*
foreman 10.4 – *Vorarbeiter*
fork-lift truck 8.3 – *Gabelstapler*
four squared (4^2) 6.3 – *vier hoch zwei, vier im Quadrat*
fraction of a second 8.1 – *Bruchteil einer Sekunde*
frequency 13.1 – *Frequenz*
friction 4.1 – *Reibung*
fridge 7.3 – *Kühlschrank*
fuel 15.4 – *Brenn-, Kraft-, Treibstoff*
fuel consumption 15.4 – *Kraftstoff-verbrauch*
full driving licence 20.2 – *Führerschein aller Klassen*
fuse 9.1 – *Sicherung*
fuse box 7.4 – *Sicherungskasten*

G

gap 8.4 – *Lücke*
gasoline 15.4 – *Benzin*
gearbox 14.2 – *Getriebe*
gearwheel 4.5 – *Getrieberad*
gender 20.2 – *Geschlecht*
generate 2.1 – *erzeugen*
ghost 14.2 – *Geist*
glass vial 18.2 – *Glasfläschchen, -ampulle*
glow 4.1 – *glühen*
graph 11.5 – *Kurve, Grafik*
ground/earth 5.1 – *Erde*

H

hairdryer 6.2 – *Fön*
halogen lamp 11.4 – *Halogenlampe*
handbook 18.5 – *Bedienungsanleitung, Handbuch*
has 1.2 – *hat*
heater 18.1 – *Heizgerät*
heavy goods vehicle driving licence 20.4 – *Lkw-Führerschein*
heavy metal 15.4 – *Schwermetall*
hedge trimmer 9.1 – *Heckenschere*
highlighted 14.1 – *hervorgehoben*
high-tension cable 7.1 – *Hochspannungs-kabel*
high-voltage 1.2 – *Hochspannungs-*
holder 12.1 – *Halter(ung)*
home charging station 14.2 – *Lade-station für zu Hause*
household 9.3 – *Haushalt; Haushalts-*
householder 18.1 – *Hauseigentümer/in*
human resources 20.1 – *Mitarbeiter, Personal(abteilung)*
hybrid vehicles 15.1 – *Hybridfahrzeug*

I

in parallel 5.4 – *parallel geschaltet*
in series 5.4 – *in Reihe geschaltet*
incandescent bulb 11.4 – *Glühbirne*
indefinitely 2.1 – *unbestimmt*
induce 3.3 – *auslösen*
inductive proximity sensor 19.1 – *induktiver Näherungssensor*
inefficient 11.1 – *ineffizient, unwirtschaftlich*
inlet valve 8.2 – *Einlassventil*
insert 12.1 – *einführen*
install 14.2 – *installieren, einrichten*
installation 10.2 – *Installation, Anlage*
installing 20.2 – *Installieren*
instructor 1.1 – *Ausbilder/in*
insulation 10.2 – *Isolierung*
intense 11.1 – *intensiv*
internal combustion engine (ICE) 15.1 – *Verbrennungsmotor*
interpreting 10.4 – *Dolmetschen*
iron 12.2 – *Eisen*

J

junction 17.1 – *Kreuzung*

K

keep clear 10.2 – *freihalten*
kick in 15.1 – *einsetzen, sich einschalten*

L

label 1.4 – *beschriften, benennen*
laboratory 11.5 – *Labor(atorium)*
lamp 7.3 – *Lampe, Leuchte*
layer 17.1 – *Schicht*
lead 2.1 – *Blei*
lead-dioxide 2.1 – *Bleidioxid*
lethal 8.1 – *tödlich*
lever 18.2 – *Hebel*
licensed 20.6 – *genehmigt, amtlich zugelassen*
light 1.2 – *Licht, Lampe, Leuchte; erleuchten*
light bulb 1.1 – *Glühbirne*
lightning 1.1 – *Blitz*
lightning strike 7.2 – *Blitzschlag*
limit 17.5 – *begrenzen*
limit switch 19.1 – *End(ab)schalter, Begrenzungsschalter*
limited 11.1 – *beschränkt, begrenzt*
lithium-ion battery 14.2 – *Lithium-Ionen-Batterie*
live (circuit) 10.1 – *stromführend (Stromkreis)*
load 1.1 – *Ladung, Last, Belastung; belasten, laden*
locate 20.1 – *platzieren, laden*
lock 10.1 – *(ab)schließen*
long(est) lasting 2.1 – *langdauernd, am längsten haltend*
looter 7.2 – *Plünderer*
lower 5.2 – *verringern*

M

magnet 3.1 – *Magnet*
magnetic field 3.1 – *Magnetfeld*
(the) mains 1.1 – *Stromnetz*
maintaining 20.2 – *Warten*
manufacturer 2.4 – *Hersteller/in*
marital status 20.2 – *Familienstand*
married 20.4 – *verheiratet*
mathematical signs 6.3 – *mathematische Zeichen*
medical use 11.1 – *medizinische Verwendung*
mercury 11.1 – *Quecksilber*
mobile 20.2 – *mobil, beweglich*
mobile phone 7.3 – *Mobiltelefon, Handy*
motivated 20.6 – *motiviert*
mounted on 12.2 – *montiert auf*
movable contact 16.1 – *beweglicher Kontakt*
movement 4.1 – *Bewegung*
MRI scanner 8.3 – *Kernspintomograph*
multimeter 10.1 – *Vielfachmess-instrument*

N

nail 12.5 – *Nagel*
name tag 19.5 – *Namensschild*
negative 1.1 – *negativ*
neutrons 1.1 – *Neutronen*
nickel 15.4 – *Nickel*
nickel-metal hydride battery 15.4 – *Nickel-(Metallhydrid)-Batterie*

O

observe 8.1 – *beachten*
office block 13.3 – *Bürogebäude, -hochhaus*
off-peak electricity 8.1 – *Strom außerhalb der Stoßzeiten*
offshore 20.1 – *vor der Küste*
onshore 20.1 – *an Land*
open loop control 18.1 – *offener Regel-kreis*
operate 8.4 – *an-, betreiben*
oppose 3.1 – *sich widersetzen*
overalls 20.7 – *Overall, Arbeitsanzug*
overhead cable 7.1 – *Überlandleitung*
overheat 9.1 – *(sich) überhitzen*
overload 9.1 – *überlasten*

P

packing station 19.1 – *Packstation*
panel 10.2 – *Anzeige-, Schalttafel*
paper clip 12.1 – *Büroklammer*
period of time 8.1 – *Zeitraum, -spanne, -abschnitt*
permanent magnet 3.5 – *permanenter Magnet*
petrol engine 15.2 – *Benzin-, Vergaser-motor*
petrol station 14.2 – *Tankstelle*
phase 13.1 – *Phase*
photovoltaic cell 2.1 – *photoelektrische Zelle*
physicist 13.2 – *Physiker/in*
placement 20.2 – *Stelle, Anstellung, Praktikum*
plastic film 19.3 – *Plastikfolie*
plastic tube 12.1 – *Plastiktube*
plate 2.3 – *Platte*
plug 9.3 – *Stecker*
plug in 7.4 – *einstöpseln, anschließen*
polarity 3.3 – *Polarität*
pole 3.5 – *Pol*
pollute 14.2 – *verschmutzen*
positive 1.1 – *positiv*
potential difference 1.1 – *Spannungsdifferenz*
power 1.1 – *Kraft, Energie, Strom; antreiben*
power company 7.2 – *Stromunternehmen*
power consumption 6.2 – *Strom-verbrauch*
power cord 14.2 – *Netz-, Stromkabel*
power cut 7.4 – *Stromausfall, -sperre, -abschaltung*
power distribution 7.1 – *Stromlieferung*
power drill 4.3 – *elektrische Bohrmaschine, Elektrobohrer*
power grid 7.2 – *Strom(versorgungs)netz*
power measuring meter 8.5 – *Strom-zähler*
power source 1.2 – *Strom-, Energiequelle*
power station 6.1 – *Kraftwerk*
power tool 4.5 – *Elektrowerkzeug, -gerät*
precaution 8.1 – *Vorsichtsmaßnahme*
presentation 4.5 – *Vorstellung, Präsen-tation*
pressure 19.1 – *Druck*
primary education 20.2 – *Grundschul (aus)bildung*
primary power 8.1 – *Primärenergie*
produce 1.1 – *produzieren, erzeugen*

production hall 19.1 – Produktionshalle
program switch 18.3 – Programmschalter
programmable logic controller (PLC) 19.1 – speicherprogrammierbare Steuerung
proton 1.1 – Proton
pump 8.1 – Pumpe; pumpen
purpose 9.4 – Zweck, Ziel
push button switch 4.5 – Druckschalter
pylon 7.1 – Mast

Q

qualified 10.3 – qualifiziert, ausgebildet
quality control department 19.5 – Qualitätskontrollabteilung

R

radio signal 5.2 – Funksignal
range 14.2 – Radius, Reichweite
RCD (residual current device) 9.1 – Fehlerstromschutzschalter
reaction 2.1 – Reaktion
receive 5.2 – empfangen
recharge 2.1 – aufladen
rechargeable batteries 2.1 – aufladbare Batterien
recording 4.4 – Aufnahme
recruiter 20.1 – Anwerber/in
recruiting 20.1 – Anwerbung
recruitment agency 20.1 – Stellen-, Arbeitsvermittlung
rectify 5.2 – berichtigen, gleichrichten
rectifying 17.1 – Gleichrichten
reduce to 7.1 – reduzieren auf
regenerative braking 14.2 – regeneratives Bremsen
register 18.1 – registrieren
regulate 13.1 – regulieren, regeln
relay 18.3 – Relais
release 8.1 – freisetzen, -geben
repairing 20.2 – Reparieren
repel 12.2 – abstoßen
reservoir 8.2 – Stausee, -becken
reset 9.1 – zurückstellen
resistance 1.1 – Widerstand
resistor 5.1 – Widerstand
restroom (AE) 19.5 – Toilette, Bad
retain 8.1 – speichern, behalten
rewirable fuse 9.1 – reparierbare Sicherung (in Deutschland unbekannt, war in England üblich)
rod 2.1 – Stab
rotate 3.1 – rotieren (lassen), drehen
rotation 8.2 – Drehung
rotor 13.1 – Rotor
rubber band 12.1 – Gummiband
rule 10.1 – Regel, Vorschrift

S

safety 10.1 – Sicherheit
safety device 9.1 – Sicherheitsvorrichtung
safety features 9.5 – Sicherheitsvorkehrungen, -merkmale
sand away 12.1 – abschleifen, abisolieren
sandpaper 12.1 – Sandpapier
schematic 17.4 – schematische Darstellung, Grafik
school leaving certificate 20.2 – (Schul-) Abschlusszeugnis, Mittlere Reife
scientist 4.1 – (Natur-)Wissenschaftler/in
seat belt 14.2 – Sicherheitsgurt
secondary education 20.2 – Sekundarstufe 1 und 2
semiconductor 17.1 – Halbleiter
sensitive 9.1 – empfindlich
sensor 18.1 – Sensor, (Mess-)Fühler
separate 1.1 – trennen
shock 10.2 – Schlag; schockieren
shop sign 4.3 – Ladenschild
short-circuit 7.4 – kurzschließen
shower 9.3 – Dusche; duschen
sign 10.2 – Schild; unterschreiben
silicon 17.1 – Silizium
skill 20.1 – Fertigkeit, Fähigkeit
socket 9.1 – Steckdose
sodium lamp– Natriumlampe
solution 8.1 – Lösung
sound 5.2 – Laut, Ton
spark 1.1 – Funke
spark plug 1.1 – Zündkerze
specifications 8.5 – (technische) Angaben
speed control unit 4.5 – Radarkontrolle, Blitzgerät
spin 12.1 – (sich) (schnell) drehen
split-ring commutator 12.2 – Stromwender (mit Stromwenderlamellen)
sports stadium 11.1 – (Sport-)Stadion
spring 16.1 – Feder
spur (circuit) 9.3 – anregen (Stromkreis)
square root 6.3 – Quadratwurzel
squirrel-cage rotor 14.1 – Käfiganker
statement 20.1 – Aussage
stationary 15.1 – stehend, im Stand
stationary contact 16.1 – feststehender Kontakt
stator 4.5 – Ständer
step up/down 7.1 – hoch/heruntertransformieren
storage power plant 8.1 – Speicherwasserkraftwerk
store 5.2 – Vorrat; speichern
storeroom 11.2 – Lagerraum
structure of the atom 4.1 – Atomstruktur
subject line 20.1 – Betreffzeile
substation 7.1 – Umspannwerk
suitable 6.6 – geeignet, passend
sulphuric acid 2.3 – Schwefelsäure
summary 6.6 – Zusammenfassung
supercapacitor 8.1 – Superkondensator
supplier 7.4 – Anbieter/in, Lieferant/in
supply 6.1 – liefern; Lieferung
survey 11.5 – Umfrage, Untersuchung; untersuchen
switch 5.1 – Schalter; (um)schalten
switchboard 5.2 – Satzbautafel
switched fused connection 9.3 – Schaltsicherung
switchgear 8.2 – Schaltgerät, -vorrichtung
switching 17.1 – (Um-)Schalten
switching unit 16.4 – (Um-)Schaltgerät
symbol 5.1 – Symbol, Zeichen

T

table 8.4 – Tabelle
tag 10.1 – kennzeichnen
tape to 12.1 – kleben an
technician 7.4 – Techniker/in
temperature 15.4 – Temperatur
terminal 1.1 – Ausgang, Anschluss
three-phase induction motor 13.1 – Drehstrom(induktions)motor
thyristor 17.1 – Thyristor
to and fro 4.1 – hin und her
toggle switch 18.1 – Kippschalter
top rates 20.6 – Spitzenlöhne, -gehälter
torch 8.1 – Taschenlampe
torque 13.3 – Drehmoment, -kraft
tough 20.6 – hart,rau
traditional 4.1 – traditionell
traffic lights 7.3 – (Verkehrs-)Ampel
trainee 1.1 – Auszubildende/r, Praktikant/in
traineeship 20.2 – Ausbildung(sverhältnis), Lehre
training 20.1 – Ausbildung, Schulung
tram 20.6 – Straßenbahn, Tramway
transformer 4.3 – Transformator
transmission line 7.2 – Übertragungsleitung
transmit 5.2 – übertragen
trip a … 9.1 – etw aktivieren
troubleshooting 16.4 – Fehlersuche
tumble dryer 6.2 – Trommeltrockner
turbine 8.2 – Turbine
turns of wire 3.5 – Drahtwindungen

U

ultrasonic sensor 19.1 – Ultraschallschalter
underground cable 7.1 – unterirdisches Kabel

V

value 1.2 – Wert
valve 18.1 – Ventil
variable capacitor 5.1 – Drehkondensator
variable frequency drive (VFD) 13.1 – Antrieb mit Frequenzumrichter
vehicle 11.1 – Fahrzeug
ventilation system 13.3 – Belüftungssystem
vessel 2.3 – Behälter
video camera 4.3 – Videokamera
voltage 1.1 – Spannung
voluntary member 20.2 – freiwilliges Mitglied

W

warehouse 16.4 – Lager(halle)
washing machine 8.5 – Waschmaschine
waste 15.1 – Verschwendung; verschwenden
water-cooled 11.1 – wassergekühlt
wattage 6.2 – Wattleistung
weak point which breaks first 9.1 – Sollbruchstelle
wheel 15.1 – Rad
windings 14.1 – Windungen
wiring system 9.3 – Verkabelung
wooden base 12.1 – Holzplatte
work out 8.5 – ausrechnen, herausfinden
work placement 9.4 – Praktikum
workmate 10.1 – Kollege
workshop 11.5 – Werkstatt, Werkshalle
wound in loops 3.1 – spiralförmig gewickelt
wrap around 12.1 – wickeln um

X

xenon short arc lamp 11.4 – Xenon-Kurzlichtbogenlampe
X-ray machine 8.3 – Röntgengerät

Z

Zener diode 17.4 – Zener-Diode
zinc 2.1 – Zink